Actes du XIVème Congrès UISPP, Université de Liège, Belgique, 2-8 septembre 2001

Acts of the XIVth UISPP Congress, University of Liège, Belgium, 2-8 September 2001

Colloque / Symposium 9.4

Le Mégalithisme Atlantique
The Atlantic Megaliths

Édité par / Edited by

Antón A. Rodriguez Casal

BAR International Series 1521
2006

Published in 2016 by
BAR Publishing, Oxford

BAR International Series 1521

Proceedings of the XIV World Congress of the IUPPS
Actes du XIV Congrès Mondial de l'UISPP

Le Mégalithisme Atlantique / The Atlantic Megaliths

ISBN 978 1 84171 958 0

© UISPP / IUPPS and the editors and contributors severally and the Publisher 2006

Avec la collaboration du Ministère de la Région Wallonne
Direction générale de l'Aménagement du territoire, du Logement et du Patrimoine
Subvention n° 04/15844

Marcel Otte, Secrétaire général du XIVème Congrès de l'U.I.S.P.P.
Université de Liège, Service de Préhistoire, 7, place du XX août, bât. A1, 4000 Liège, Belgique
Tél. 0032/4/366.53.41 Fax 0032/4/366.55.51 Email : prehist@ulg.ac.be
Web : http://www.ulg.ac.be/prehist

Editing : Rebecca Miller
Typesetting and layout: Darko Jerko

The authors' moral rights under the 1988 UK Copyright,
Designs and Patents Act are hereby expressly asserted.

All rights reserved. No part of this work may be copied, reproduced, stored,
sold, distributed, scanned, saved in any form of digital format or transmitted
in any form digitally, without the written permission of the Publisher.

BAR Publishing is the trading name of British Archaeological Reports (Oxford) Ltd.
British Archaeological Reports was first incorporated in 1974 to publish the BAR
Series, International and British. In 1992 Hadrian Books Ltd became part of the BAR
group. This volume was originally published by Archaeopress in conjunction with
British Archaeological Reports (Oxford) Ltd / Hadrian Books Ltd, the Series principal
publisher, in 2006. This present volume is published by BAR Publishing, 2016.

Printed in England

BAR titles are available from:

                BAR Publishing
                122 Banbury Rd, Oxford, OX2 7BP, UK
EMAIL   info@barpublishing.com
PHONE +44 (0)1865 310431
  FAX   +44 (0)1865 316916
            www.barpublishing.com

TABLE DES MATIÈRES / TABLE OF CONTENTS

An Introduction to the Atlantic Megalithic Complex 1
A.A. Rodríguez Casal

The Megalithic Complex in Cantabrian Spain 11
P. Arias, A. Armendariz & L. C. Teira

Le phénomène funéraire dans le Pays Basque pendant le Néolithique
    et l'age des métaux : contextes culturels 31
J. Fernandez Eraso & J.A. Mujika Alustiza

On the Life-Histories of Megaliths in Northwest Iberia 43
M. Martinón-Torres

Research on the Megalithic Culture of Galicia (NW Iberian Peninsula)
    During the Last Century 53
A.A. Rodríguez Casal

AN INTRODUCTION TO THE ATLANTIC MEGALITHIC COMPLEX

Antón A. RODRÍGUEZ CASAL

1. SOME METHODOLOGICAL ISSUES

When I first presented to the UISPP the proposal of a colloquium on the Atlantic Megalithic Complex, my idea was a discussion of general issues regarding this phenomenon across such a distinctive area, as a continuation of the conference held in Santiago de Compostela in 1996 under the topic "The Atlantic Neolithic and the Origins of Megaliths". In the end, the scope of the colloquium was constrained to a much more precise region, that is the Cantabrian coast, between Galicia and the Basque Country, an area under the joint influences of the European North, the interior of the Iberian Peninsula, and Portugal. Even if less known, this region is not unimportant. On the contrary, in the last few years it has become the focus of increasing research interest, as shown by the contributions presented here, by authors from Galicia (Martinón-Torres and Rodríguez Casal), from the University of Cantabria (Arias Cabal, Teira and Armendáriz) and Basque researchers (Fernández Eraso and Mújica).

The Megalithic Complex must be considered a universal and versatile phenomenon, the product of a complex series of interactions developing from the fifth millenium BC, as a response to the economic and social readjustment subsequent to the climatic crisis of the end of the Pleistocene. Mesolithic groups, agricultural societies, colonisation of new spaces, emergence of new social structures... all these are underlying factors of a transcultural phenomenon which, along the Atlantic coast, materialised in the megalithic monuments.

Undoubtedly, the Megalithic Complex is one of the facets of Prehistory that has given rise to more academic interest. However, many crucial questions remain open. This is particularly true in an area such as the Cantabrian coast, traditionally considered as marginal.

Several decades ago, Professor Glyn Daniel wondered: Which ancient populations built the megalithic tombs, in which ancient European settings and why? Notwithstanding the difficulties of answering these questions, the following papers present an attempt to address the who, where, when and why of the development of the megalithic phenomenon, making special emphasis on the following aspects:

a) The megalithic architecture as a foundation of the archaeological study, paying attention to the outstanding polymorphism in terms of construction plans, setting patterns and burial rituals.

b) The analysis of the spatial distribution of this phenomenon, in a well-defined geographic area such as the Atlantic coast of Europe.

c) On this basis, identification of continuities and singularities across the region of study, with a special interest in aspects such as the process of diffusion, acculturation phenomena or convergence of forms, diversity and cohesion.

From this perspective, it will be possible to understand the existence (or lack therein) of cultural filiation, regional contacts or diffusion of stimuli, or why the presence of identical architectural solutions in distant geographic areas may be the result of independent inventions, in contrast with outdated migration and diffusion theories.

As regards the terminology, the Megalithic Complex is often defined as a cultural (or rather, transcultural) phenomenon, whose most characteristic external feature is the construction of funerary and/or ritual monuments with large stones. The term monument is used insofar as, besides the funerary one, the architecture plays an important role in the ritual complex. This is mostly evident in the big cairns or long barrows of the British Isles or the West of France, in which the external structure is composed of an arrangement of well carved stones with reinforcements and steps, with a fuction that clearly goes beyond the mere technical support to incorporate ritual issues such as the marking of a sacred space or an external social identification. Understood in this manner, the monument may function, in some cases, as a point of reference for a social group, or as a mark of territory.

In spite of the use of the adjective "megalithic", it is worth noting that not all the monuments were built with large stones: this is the case, for example, of the false dome monuments or *tholoi* (thus named because of their similarity with the large mycenic constructions), built with dry stone walls. Usual terms to refer to megalithic monuments in the Spanish archaeological literature are *túmulo*, *dólmen*, *galería cubierta*, etc; or, to use the authors's Galician language, *mámoa*, *medorra*, *medoña*, *arca*, *anta* and their derivatives.

2. MEGALITHIC SPACES IN THE EUROPEAN ATLANTIC COAST

This geographic space spans from the Northwest of Europe – including the North Sea, the English Channel, South Scandinavia, Denmark and North Germany –, to the

Southwest, down to the Southern regions of the Iberian Peninsula. In this Atlantic space, the ocean imposes a new way of thinking and living, different from that of the inlands. Here, the building of megalithic monuments goes hand in hand with the renewed worldview of the first farmers of Western Europe. The characterisation of this complex phenomenon remains a challenge for modern scholars.

Originally, the formal similarities amongst the monuments of different regions gave rise to claims of an only origin in the Eastern Mediterranean for the whole megalithic phenomenon. This led to the unquestioned acceptance of the now outdated *ex Oriente lux* theory, based on migrationist/diffusionist assumptions. For some scholars, such as Bosch Gimpera, the region embracing North Portugal and Galicia could be the "birthplace" of the Megalithic Complex; for others; more recently, this honour would be held by Brittany. Nowadays we know, however, that several indepentent "inventions" took place more or less synchronically (see below).

Yet more original theories exist, such as that of Savory, based on the assumption of large scale direct contacts amongst the different "ends of the world" or *finisterrae*, which led him to suggest the existence of actual maritime routes. As Giot would ironically state, "with some more imagination we would end up envisaging the monuments themselves proudly navigating across the ocean". Other purely speculative theories are those by Jiménez del Oso, Von Daniken or E. Mackie, and a long list of gullible archaeoastronomers, founded on the unsubstantiated theories of authors such as L.V. Grinssel, D.C. Heggie, A. Thom o M. Brennan.

This explanatory effervescence changed dramatically with the publication of a series of radiocarbon dates that clashed with traditional schemes of cultural evolution. This new scenario saw the publication of new, polycentrist theories to explain the origins of megaliths. The main representatives of this school of thought would be Glyn Daniel, Pierre Roland Giot and Colin Renfrew, amongst others.

I often quote Professor Giot who, on the occasion of the First Atlantic Colloquium held in Britanny in 1961, referred to the Atlantic coast as a zone encompassing a range of contemporaneous civilisations, each of them with specific regional qualities, but all of them sharing some features. This underlying idea will lead this paper to the discussion of those singularities mentioned by Professor Giot, but also of the possible reasons behind the varying megalithic architectures. Before attempting any interpretation let us, therefore, present an overview of the megalithic areas in Atlantic Europe.

Northwest Europe

Two distinct areas may be mentioned: on the one hand, Southern Scandinavia, Denmark, Polland, Northern Germany and Holland; on the other hand, the British Isles.

As an indication of the importance of the first, vast region, one may recall Ebbesen's 1985 estimate of the number of preserved megaliths in **Denmark**: no less than 7,000!, and it is possible that more than 20,000 were originally built. One of the most intrinsic features of these megaliths is that they were built with natural stone slabs, vestiges of Pleistocene Glaciations. These monuments appear related to those of Southern **Sweden**, studied by authors such as G. Burenhult, L. Kaelas or M. Strömberg. On the continent, some of the most outstanding examples are the *Hunenbedden* of **Holland** (burials with a side entrance, like those from Brittany) or the *Steinkisten* in Northern **Germany**, with elongated tumuli, proto-dolmens, rectangular chambers, passage dolmens and cists, masterly studied by E. Sprockhoff in his *Die Nordische Megalithkultur*.

Given its originality, it is worth highlighting the megalithic phenomenon in the **British Isles**, with separated nuclei in Irland, on the one hand, and, Western England, Wales and, above all, Scotland, on the other hand.

Scotland is a crucial centre of megalithic development, with over 400 passage domens, first studied systematically by Henshall. The megalithic phenomenon is particularly spectacular in archipelagos such as the Hebrides, Shetland and, above all, the Orkney Islands, including such renowned sites as Maes Howe, with its peculiar burials consisting of a square chamber with buttresses, dry stone walls and false domes. This constructive system is to be found in Southern Portugal, namely in the necropolis of Alcalar, although here with circular chambers. The parallel, although distant in space and remarkably different in the associated material culture and ritual, led some to dream of direct maritime megalithic relationships. In actual fact, these "non megalithic" constructions should be understood as a result of the lack of large stone slabs on the islands. As suggested by C. Richards, these innovative constructions evolved from a domestic architectural tradition, present in Neolithic villages such as well-known Scara Brae. But other elements clearly link these islands with continental Scotland, and even with Brittany: this is the case of the "multiperiod chambered long cairns", which R. Joussaume relates to similar constructions in the Centre-West of France, despite their geographic distance: over 2,000 km!

In the southern regions of Great Britain, it is worth mentioning the cluster of Severn-Cotswold-tombs, with simple burials (normally in areas with Mesoithic sites) as well as large monuments such as West Kennet. In **Wales**, the Bryn-Celli-Ddu mound stands out because of its monumentality and, confined to British *finisterrae*, the megaliths in **Cornwall** and the small passage tombs of the **Isles of Scilly.**

Although closer to the continent, and already in the area of influence of Brittany, the megalithic group of the Channel Islands is of interest, especially the large tumulus of Hougue Bie, almost 60 m in diameter, and sites such as Les Fouaillages in Guernesey, dated to the beginnings of the fifth millennium BC.

One of the most original centres of the Atlantic Megalithic Complex is Ireland, with over 1,200 megaliths and four main typological groups: court-tombs, portal-tombs, wedge-tombs and passage-tombs. Well documented thanks to the work by G. Eogan, E. Shee, M. Herity, M. O'Kelly and S. Bergh, some of the most important sites are Carrowkeel, Fourknoks, Loughhcrew, Carrowmore or, above all, the Boyne valley, with very famous monuments such as Dowth, Knowth or Newgrange.

On the origins of Irish megaliths, theories vary between independent invention and diffusion. The latter interpretation presents the Irish megalithic phenomenon as ultimately dependant of either Northern Europe (Scandinavia) or – more frequently – Armorica. According to the radiocarbon dates, the origins of the phenomenon date to ca. 3500 BC, that is later than the older megaliths of Britain or the Atlantic coast of the Iberian Peninsula. However, A. Apsimon places the beginnings of the Irish megaliths in the period 4000-3800 BC, with portico barrows, followed in 3850-3500 BC with patio barrows, and passage graves from 2500 BC, whose origins would be in Britain.

Atlantic France

From North to South, three large regions should be outlined: Normandy, Brittany and Centre-West, with connections to Belgium in the North, and to Gironde and the Iberian Peninsula in the South.

Important monuments of varied typology are found in **Normandy**. Some of the most remarkable are the cairns of La Hogue and La Hoguette, with collective burials in passage graves with false domes. Given its geographic location, cultural influences may come from the East (Danubian culture) as much as from the **Armorica**, a fundamental region in the genesis of Atlantic megaliths.

Monuments such as Carnac, Locmariaquer, Barnenez or Gavrinis are just a few examples of the megalithic wealth of **Brittany**, with thousands of barrows and menhirs, amongst which the extraordinary cluster of alignments in Carnac may be highlighted. Another group of special relevance is that of the large mounds of Carnac (the largest being St.-Michel, with 125 m). According to Briard, these are "testimonies of an extraordinary and colossal architecture, left by an organised and clearly hierarchical society."

Undeniably, this is one of the places where the European megalithic complex was invented, which is proved by the very early dates of some monuments, pointing to the fifth millenium BC. Most remarkable are passage graves, with false dome or monolithic covers, placed within small mounds or huge cairns, of which Barnenez is a paradigmatic example: with its 70 m in the longest axis, 5 m in height and containing 11 passage graves with masonry and dry stone walls. Placed on the coast, overlooking the Morlaix bay, Barnenez has been described by J. Briard as a tomb on the sea, "a funerary ship travelling to the West beyond the Ocean, towards the other world".

Another element of this region to be noted is the existence of extraordinary rock art, with Gavrinis as a *chef d'oeuvre*, playing a role similar to that of Newgrange or Knowth in Ireland. This is another factor that culturally links Armorica to Ireland, or even to the Iberian Peninsula, as expounded by E. Shee Twoigh (1981). Burials, menhirs and steles thus form a living world deeply engrained in a funerary worship, in which some standing stones were pulled down in order to build collective burials for the ancestors, as splendidly described by Jean L'Helgouac'h in his paper "Les idoles qu'on abatte." This demonstrates that shrines with steles such as Locmariaquer are older than passage graves, as shown in Gavrinis or Table des Marchands.

Towards the South of Brittany, the Loira region preserves interesting vestiges of the Megalithic Complex, such as the sites of Dissignac or Les Mousseaux, which form a cultural entity with Vendée and **Charente-Poitou** in the Centre-West, a region open to several influences, related to Armorica, the Southern Chasseense, Central France and the Paris basin.

With such representative examples as Les Cous, Bénon, La Boixe, Champ Chalon or Bougon, the megaliths of the latter region include elongated mounds with a chamber, Carnac-style mounds, passage barrows and some local types such as the so-called Angevine portico barrows, Angoumousine barrows or the covered galleries. Chronologically, the fist megaliths seem to appear in the Middle Neolithic, ca. 4500-4000 BC. Even though the megalithic phenomenon in the Centre-West was once seen as marginal in relation to Brittany, nowadays the singularities of that region are highlighted, as are some of the radiocarbon dates, comparable to those from Brittany, for example monument F0 in Bougon.

Aquitaine, in the Soutwest, is another region that appears in the traditional archaeological literature as marginal. Nowadays, megaliths in this area are better known after the work by M. Roussot-Larroque and M. Devignes. From the Gironde estuary to the Spanish Basque Country, simple dolmens and long barrows have been catalogued, similar to other Basque and Pyrenean examples, as well as large mounds with passage graves that may be compared to others in the Cantabrian coast of the Iberian Peninsula.

The Iberian Peninsula

Having overcome the historiographic tension between "Orientalist" and "Occidentalist" theories, the Iberian Peninsula must now be considered as the area where two influences interact, one Atlantic, the other one Mediterranean. The Mediterranean is the quiet sea, the *Mer Partagée*, as described by Jean Guilaine. Facing it, the Atlantic Ocean, fierce and ungovernable, with several *finisterrae* from the Orkney Islands to Cape of San Vicente. Between Atlantic and Mediterranean, Iberia appers as the crucible were tensions are attenuated and cultures are blended. This is the only perspective that allows an understanding of the extreme polymorfism of the Iberian megaliths, the variety of architectural solutions, the remarkable difference in grave goods and, altogether, the various rituals of collective burial. The Atlantic-Mediterranean tension, on the one hand, and the climatic and geographic diversity, on the other hand, will model the megalithic landscape across Iberia.

The problem of the origins of megaliths in the Iberian Peninsula is one of the longest-standing questions. After a long and fruitless clash between "Occidentalists", led by P. Bosch Gimpera, and "Orientalists", following M. Almagro Basch, researchers progressively acepted the possibility that several cultural traditions may have existed, and even an independent invention of the megalithic phenomenon in Iberia. The matter, however, is not fully resolved. In this sense, it is worth remembering Professor Glyn Daniel's statement, citing Gordon Childe over twenty years ago: "If you can offer a satisfactory explanation for the origins of megaliths in Iberia, you will hold the key to all the megalithic problems."

Galicia and the Cantabrian coast, between France and Portugal

This study area spans from the Northwest of Iberia to the region of the gulf of Gasconia. It comprises the regions of Galicia, Asturias, Cantabria and the Basque Country. The intensity of research has been rather unequal across the different geographic units.

The Westernmost region, Galicia, is an ancient massif characterised by an abundance of valleys and rivers, with a particularly steep coast. The second region considered, i.e. Asturias and the area of the Central Cantabrian coast, comprises several well-defined areas: a narrow costal plain, a series of coastal mountain ranges, a pre-coastal depression and, to the south, the Picos de Europa, which reach 2500 m. in heigth and separate this region from the Spanish plateau. Finally, the Basque Country includes two geographic, climatic, and sometimes culturally, delimited entities, separated by the watershed of the Atlantic Ocean and the Mediterranean Sea.

Towards the fourth millennium BC., the ritual of collective burial in barrows with simple chambers and passage graves was spread in the Northwest of the Iberian Península. The barrows are normally small and sometimes show internal structures with lithic cuirasses and rings of stones. Entrance passages do not appear until a later stage. Towards the end of the Megalithic Complex we find smaller tombs (cist type) and even individual burial pits, which announce the individual burials typical of the Bell Beakers and Bronze Age cultures. As to artistic expressions, around 30 megalithic monuments with carvings and paintings have been catalogued. The artistic repertoire is completed by idols with and without decoration, together with antrhropomorphic steles. Among the most relevant sites we could highlight the monuments of Dombate and Parxubeira, together with the necrópolis of Monte de Santa Mariña, Monte Penido, Terra Cha or Leboreiro and Maus de Salas.

From the last comprehensive study of sthe megalithic complex in the Cantabrian region, conducted by P. Arias, L. Teira and A. Armendáriz, more than 1250 monuments – menhirs and, above all, megalithic tombs - are known in the area. They appear distributed following a relatively uniform pattern throughout the landscape, from de coast up to the high interior mountains. The Cantabrian megalithic tombs are simple and small in size, even though there are some exceptions. Some or their slabs show artistic expresssions. Radiocarbon dating suggests that most of the monuments were built towards the end of the fifth and the first half of the fourth millennium BC. The grave goods, however, reveal that the tombs were used at least until the third millennium cal BC.

Like in Galicia, the most reliable data from Asturias and Cantabria hint at an emergence of the megalithic culture and the funerary ritual of collective burial in a variety of tomb types (passage dolmens or simple polygonal chambers), placed in monumental settings. In addition, there are a few anthropological remains in caves, together with other exceptional pieces of evidence. The most usual ritual would be the burial, given that the charcoal recovered at the excavations should never be interpreted as evidence of cremation.

In the Basque Country, some elements point to the use of caves as graves, although the data regarding funeray rituals are scarce. In Marizulo cave, particularly in the level I, two burials were discovered. The former was an individual cist formed by three slabs, associated to sheep and dog remains, and dated to the fifth millennium BC, whereas the latter, more recent in time, was a collective burial. In other caves such as Santimamiñe, Lumentxa, Atxeta, Abtiaga, Kobeaga or Urtiaga, human remains have also been recovered. The ritual of collective burial during the Megalithic Complex is almost the only source of information regarding the use of monuments in mountain landscapes (mainly simple dolmens). On the other hand, grave goods are rare and bone remains almost inexistent. In the dolmen of Ausokoi, eleven individuals were identified. Also the barrows of Sierra de Aralar should be highlighted, with up to one hundred burials. In Urtao II cave, a synchronic episode of collective burial of around fifty individuals was identified.

In the Southern regions of the Basque Country, besides the ritual of burial in passage graves, the most important information comes from caves or collective pits such as that of San Juan Ante Portam Latinam. Here, a "simultaneous múltiple burial type" was defined. The research directed by archaeologists such as J. Fernández Eraso and J. Mujica has allowed the identification of a series of monuments typologically different, which appear within the same chronological ranges. This suggests the coexistence of different types of burial, instead of a succession of types related to particular time periods. According to Eraso and Mujica, the bests known types are:

1) Pit burials in caves or shelters, and burials in the open air;

2) Surface deposits, cists in natural refuges, dolmens and cists in the open air.

And to the South: Portugal

There is an obvious continuity from Galicia towards the South, both in the landscape and in the cultural evolution, as seen in their similar megalithic types. Between the **Miño** river and the **Duero** river, the work carried out by Professor V. Oliveira Jorge since the early eighties has showed the cluster of A Aboboreira as one of the most important. Still, even more monumental are the megaliths in the Portuguese region of **Beiras**, with such famous dolmens as Carapito, Orca das Seixas or Orca dos Juncais, as well as rock art, both engravings and paintings in the so-called "Grupo de Viseu", currently under revision.

In **Centre-South** of Portugal, the Lisboa region stands out because of its architectural variety, where actual megalithic monuments co-exist with burials in natural or artificial caves or false dome burials (absent in the Iberian Peninsula and up to the French Centre-West). Thus the complexity of sites such as Praia das Maçãs, with an occidental chamber, tholos, passage and hall. Towards the interior, one cannot fail to mention the exceptional monumental concentrations in the Alentejo region, in what truly seems a home for the Atlantic megalithic phenomenon, with magnificent clusters such as Nisa-Crato, Pavia, Evora, Reguengos de Monsaraz and Ourique. To the South, in the Algarve, we find cist-type burials and small megaliths, as well as important necropoleis such as Alcalar, with a dozen tholoi. The latter, with their constructive system (dry stone and cover in false dome) were a perfect fit for diffusionists and neodiffusionists, which found here a geographic step between the alleged Oriental prototypes and similar monuments in Brittany or the British Isles.

3. ORIGINS AND DEVELOPMENT OF THE ATLANTIC MEGALITHIC COMPLEX

Leaving aside the debate between "orientalists" and "occidentalists", it is worth paying attention to the evolution in the theoretical standpoint of one of the most reputed specialists on megaliths, i.e. Professor Glyn Daniel, who departed from diffusionist assumptions, but progressively moved to polygenetic theories, on the basis of the fundamental research carried out since the fifties and the information provided by radiocarbon dating. In this way, from his theory of the "double colonisation", he would have to revise his earlier statements to the point of, in 1980, acknowledging: "I am thus compelled to conclude that chamber tombs originated independently in at least seven zones of Europe: South Spain, Portugal, Brittany, North France, North Germany, Scandinavia, South England and Wales." Along similar lines, Professor Giot had written in 1976: "in fact, at the current moment, we have evidence that similar monuments would have existed at different locations of the Atlantic coast, all of them at relatively early times."

Even if not as optimistic as Professor Daniel, I will now refer to two geographic areas, Armorica and Central Portugal, with a very early megalithic phenomenon and a very similar evolution. This will serve as an introduction to the genesis and development of the Atlantic Megalithic Complex, in which the Cantabrian coast will be necessarily included.

Armorica, cradle of Atlantic megalithic phenomenon

When addressing the topics of the origins of megaliths in this region, it is necessary to consider the relationships between megalith builders and previous Mesolithic indigenous populations. From this perspective, the small islets of Téviec and Hoëdic become relevant, in that small burials covered by a small heap of stones, in the way of small cairns, were recorded, together with remains of fire, shell and epipaleolithic tools, dating to the mid fifth millennium BC. Already in the seventies, authors such as H. Case considered these small funerary structures as proto-dolmens, a prelude of the large Armorican megalithic monuments.

More recently, scholars such as N. Cauwe have tracked the origins of megaliths further back into the past, namely to the Magdalenian Period. According to him, the contacts between hunters and farmers would have been the catalyst for the development of the great architecture in stone. This seems, however, a rather overstated hypothesis.

The archaeological evidence suggests that Mesolithic groups from the coast progressively colonised the hinterland and made contact with the first neolithic farmers of Brittany. As a result of this interchange, Mesolithic peoples would have adopted the new domestic production system, and neolithic populations would have adopted the funerary ritual exemplified by the small cairns of Téviec and Hoëdic. This is the model proposed, for example, by J. Hibbs, who thus sees no break between Mesolithic and neolithic groups. According to him, this acculturation would have taken place very swiftly. Perhaps more difficult to explain would be the almost immediate transition from the small cairns to the monumental passage graves.

In order to explain the emergence of this monumentality, and avoiding the traditional diffusionist explanations, one can resort to the idea originally proposed by C. Renfrew, that is, the existence of factors operating locally. From this vantagepoint, the phenomenon would have taken place in different regions or centres as a result of factors that may vary from one to another, and irrespective of whether contacts existed between them. In other words, the funerary practice involving the construction of megaliths could have originated independently in areas were human groups achieved similar levels of cultural evolution.

For the specific case of Armorica, the factors explaining this development could be sought in the peculiarities of the Neolithic period in Brittany, a region were agriculture and farming appear very early. The subsequent sedentism, together with technological and economic improvements, would progressively bring an important demographic growth. The monuments would make it possible for families or larger groups to encompass all of their burials within the same building, as explained by L'Helgouach'h.

An alternative explanation has gained recognition in the last few years: this is the "Danubian thesis", which would see the origins of megaliths in Central Europe. Monumental clusters such as the Passy group (Yonne), large necropolis of Danubian farmers, with approximately thirty huge mounds and pit burials, indicate that complex and hierarchical societies existed in this area as early as the fifth millennium BC! For some authors, these would be the precursors of the large Atlantic cairns and the early monuments of Western Europe. Thus Passy would represent the preceding steps for large mounds such as those in Balloy (Seine-et-Marne) or Butte de Houx, Rots or Colombiers (Normandy), as well as the large Norman cairns of La Hogue and La Hoguette, or even the Armorican ones.

The main challenge for this interpretation is the need of accurate dates. It is not clear whether the Passy group is truly earlier than the first Atlantic megaliths, as noted by C. Masset in 1993 or, more recently, by P. Van Berg. Whatever the case, contacts between the Danube and the Atlantic have occurred, as demonstrated in Lower Normandy or in Armorican sites such as St. Just, excavated by C.-T. Le Roux and J. Briard, where a mid-fifth-millennium pit burial was identified in association with ceramics of the Chambon type, that is the Danubian type of Central France.

Summarising, it seems plausible that the Atlantic megaliths saw their origins in Téviec and Hoëdic: a cultural process would have led to the evolution from the shell-midden and the protodolmen to the large cairn. However, some questions remain, for example: why did the subsequent monumentalisation did not take place in these islets, but in the Armorican peninsula? As regards the Danubian thesis, a progression from East to West could be accepted, from the Passy group towards the Western cairns, but only once the chronological uncertainties are resolved. As J. Guilaine put it in 1998: "to the thesis of an architectural model diffused from the East, another thesis can be opposed, claiming an independent genesis for the monumentality, multiform and intrinsically Occidental."

One of the research priorities at this point should be the in-depth study of internal dynamics of specific sites, beyond simplistic and overarching explanations. Paradigmatic examples are Barnenez or the large mound of Petit Monz in Arzon (Morbihan), with succeeding additions from an original tumulus to the final complexity. These cases allow an explanation of the megalithic phenomenon based on a simple juxtaposition, from domestic constructions and simple pits through earth mounds and up to well structured cairns. This reconstruction would not need theories based in evolutionary sequences from the Mesolithic to the Neolithic in the Danube.

Along these lines, the renowned specialist Jean L'Helgouac'h presented his hypotehsis at the 1996 colloquium in Santiago de Compostela, posing the very feasible possibility that the origins of megaliths in Britanny might be completely unrelated to indigenous antecedents (such as Téviec and Hoëdic) or external influences (from the Danube). According to him, the explanation would be as follows: following the implantation of agricultural groups in the early Neolithic, mostly on the south coast of Armorica, societies would steadily become wealthier and more hierarchical, which would lead to the construction of monuments as an expression of power and authority. From Brittany, the new ritual of collective burials would irradiate towards North and South. The megaliths in Normandy would thus be an import of Britanny, whilst the monuments in the Centre-West would also derive from Armorica.

The above theory, however, is not accepted by all. R. Joussaume suggests that the monuments of Passy could be the prototypes for the cairns with passage dolmens in the Centre-West, from where they would be imported into Brittany and even to the Iberian Peninsula. The origins of the collective burial could be found in the French Midi, in Epicardial contexts (Montbolo group). A relevant example could be the cave of Belesta, in the Eastern Pyrenees, with collective burials and a chronology comparable to that of Bougon F0 (ca. 3530 BC). In a ritual sense, the megalith would thus be the Atlantic counterpart of the Mediterranean cave.

What seems undeniable is that the Megalithic Complex shows an extraordinary character in the Atlantic regions of France, with Brittany as the most remarkable focus, where a great variety of rituals and constructions are recorded, resulting from multiple and successive influences stemming from various cultural traditions. As aptly argued by L. Laporte and C. T. Le Roux, the West of France is a place for synthesis but also proof of the creativity of very dynamic cultures.

Portugal in the genesis of the Megalithic Complex of the Iberian Peninsula

In order to answer questions regarding the Megalithic Culture in Portugal, one must first consider the role played by Mesolithic groups, as G. Clark pointed out years ago in his "Mesolithic Prelude". Data collected from the famous shell-middens of Muge or from Sado Valley, where dwellings and individual graves of more than 200 inhumations have been found, are pivotal here. Despite the fact that, for authors like Roche and Veiga Ferreira, Mesolithic groups from Muge might have remained outside neolithisation processes, the discovery of ceramics in superior layers of the shell-middens of Moita do Sebastião and Cabeço de Amoreira would indicate contact with neolithic groups or, in any case, "symptoms" of neolithization at a moment in which shell-middens were still being used , as originally proposed by Arnaud and Cunha Serrão in the late seventies.

The absolute chronology (from the mid sixth millennium to the end of the fourth) and the existence of ceramics suggest that the final occupation of shell-middens is contemporaneous with some neolithic sites, such as the Cave of Salemas, whose third layer was radiocarbon-dated to 4730 BC. It is not clear when the first neolithic elements emerged, how the contact between the indigenous populations and Mesolithic groups occurred, or how the megalithic phenomenon originated. To answer these questions we ought to keep in mind the early neolithisation in the Alentejo and the Portuguese Estremadura. Nevertheless, the Early Neolithic Period has been dated to ca. 4700-4000 BC, which corresponds to the "Vale Pincel I Horizon" (named after the investigations in the Vale Pincel), Vale Vistoso, Salemas and Samouqueira sites. Despite this information, we are unsure about how the neolithisation developed in Portugal. In 1982, Arnaud proposed two alternative models based on an analysis of the territory and its exploitation.

According to the first model, a process of acculturation could have occurred, along the lines of the "frontier concept" proposed by Alexander in 1977. In the second model, the appearance of neolithic technology would have been brought about by an inadequacy of the resources to meet social needs at a moment in which Mesolithic groups had already experienced full neolithisation.

What is evident is that an important event occurred in the Middle Neolithic Period: the fertile fields on the banks of the Muge were abandoned and the interior lands of the Alentejo were steadily occupied, perhaps because an increase in sea level caused flooding of the Tajo River and its tributaries, as described by Daveau in 1980. From this moment, new economic needs and social changes caused by this event may explain the appearance of the first settlements in the Alentejo and the first single burial cists at Montemor-o-Novo, Coruche and Mora, marking a penetration of neolithic groups towards the interior across the most important hydrographic basins.

The first megalithic graves, individual tombs without passages and with few grave goods (microliths, axe-heads and a virtual absence of ceramics) appear at this moment. These monuments that seem to mark the beginning of the Megalithic Complex in Portugal have been included in the proto-megalithic phase by Cunha Serrâo in 1979.

Nevertheless, Ph. Kalb has criticised this theory on the basis of her analyses of soil samples, as she considers that it would be illogical for Mesolithic groups from Muge to move to an area where the land was not suitable for agriculture. Kalb's view fails to take into account that these groups might have been forced to abandon the lands of Muge and that, moreover, that there are examples of human populations who have settled in lands ill-suited for intensive agriculture (such as populations in the Sines area whose economies were fundamentally based on marine resources and seasonal pastoralism).

A similar process with simple dolmens at the beginning of the megalithic phenomenon is evident in other Atlantic regions such as in the Northeast of the Peninsula, the Beiras, Alentejo or the Algarve. Specifically in the latter region, in Caldas de Monchique, the process was initiated by single burial cists which were succeeded by others with short entrance passages: such is the case of the Buço Preto 7 grave. On the other hand, in the necropolis of Palmeira, tombs evolved from initial oval pits up to large burials reaching a length of 6 m. An evolution such as this could have been the result of new funerary needs caused by the appearance of collective inhumation.

In the Middle Neolithic, the existence of the ritual of collective burials has been archaeologically proven in Portugal, beginning with short-passage graves (contemporaries of Buço Preto 7 or the necropolis of Palmeira) such as those of Anta 2 of Gorginos and Anta 1 of Poço da Gateira, dated by TLM to 4400 ± 360 BC and 4510 ± 360 BC. In conventional radiocarbon chronology, the tombs would be situated at the beginning of the fourth millennium at a time very similar to that of the most ancient Breton passage graves.

This phase (Megalithic 1) includes offerings of the Neolithic tradition without the presence of engraved slate plaques, a typical artefact of the great passage graves of the Alentejo which were contemporaries of the passage graves of the Beiras.

At the height of the Megalithic Culture of the Alentejo (Megalithic 2), we note the appearance of the first fortified settlements and an occupation of the Alentejan territory. At this moment, collective burials were already occurring in the Tagus estuary, in megaliths or in natural caves.

Facts such as these lead the author to believe that the neolithic reutilisation of caves in Estremadura are contemporaneous with the long passage graves of Ribatejo and the Upper Alentejo: this conclusion is based on radiocarbon dates and the similarities in the archaeological materials recovered.

The first rock-cut tombs originated at the end of the fourth millennium, although we have only one date of reference (Carenque 2 : 5880 ± 340 BP, similar to that of level b of Lapa do Fumo). No doubt, rock-cut tombs of Estremadura were continuosly reutilised from the time of their initial occupation to the Bell Beaker Culture. Different phases of occupation have been identified: Firstly, a phase where grave goods are associated to materials from the Megalithic Complex of the Alentejo, as is demonstrated by an identical microlithic industry, a scarcity of polished axes, and the presence of globular and spherical ceramic forms, as well as an absence of carinated forms. The following phase, whose prototype is the "western chamber" of the Praia das Maças, is marked by the existence of trapezoid arrow heads, segmented cylindrical bone pin-heads and engraved slate plaques. The third phase of occupation is included in the so-called "Importation Horizon", characterised by the appearance of bone bowls, concave-based arrow heads, channeled ware, dented rims and carinated forms. According to Veiga Ferreira and Leitâo, this phase coincides with the first tholos tombs; similarly, the excavations of Marques Gonçalves in the Praia das Maças have shown that the tholoi were constructed during the transition from the second to the third phase. Lastly, the rock-cut tombs of Estremadura had been reutilized in the Bell-beaker Period.

In the current state of research, it cannot be maintained that rock-cut tombs were the product of the degeneration of tholoi nor are they a late manifestation of the Megalithic Culture that originated in the Mediterranean. Thus, authors such as Whitehouse o Guilaine have already demonstrated how central Mediterranean rock-cut tombs were the result of local evolution beginning in the Middle Neolithic Period.

The appearance of tholoi in Portugal has always been a controversial subject. Traditionally, these were ascribed to the Copper Age and linked to the Importation Horizon, as a result of colonisation from the Southeastern peninsula and, originally, the eastern Mediterranean. However, this theory has been questioned. After A. Arribas' and F. Molina's excavations in the Castillejos (Granada), it has been proved that the site does not originate from the "Culture of Almería" and Los Millares group. Both authors consider that the Megalithic Period of Granada originates from the Lower Guadalquivir and even from the Alentejo, ruling out an Eastern origin.

Although the classic diffusion concept is not accepted at the present time, the emergence of the tholos tombs or metallurgy in the Iberian Peninsula should be understood in the light of local cultural traditions, without ruling out the possibility of a transfer of ideas in a "culture creep" sense described by Evans in 1956, or as discussed by G.Delibes and M. Fernández Miranda in 1985.

In order to gain an understanding of the chronology and cultural context of the Portuguese tholos tombs within the Megalithic Culture, it is important to analyse the areas in which these appear in more detail, areas which are not homogeneous but where regional characteristics are more than evident.

Traditionally, false dome tombs of Estremadura have been included in the Chalcolithic Period (tholos phase 2) and, more recently, they have been included in the transition to the Copper Age. The cases of Praia das Maçãs and Pai Mogo are particularly interesting because their stratigraphic evidence is fundamental to the understanding of the origin of the tholos tombs in the region.

Regarding Praia das Maçâs, it is noteworthy that the monument is a rock-cut tomb with dry-stone walls and not a tholos tomb in a strict sense. Furthermore, after Marques Gonçalves' excavations, the similarity of grave goods from the so-called tholos to those from the Late Neolithic Period has been proved.

With regard to the tholos tomb of Pai Mogo, an earlier occupation before the Importation Horizon appears to be evident as a result of the archaeological data: objects such as green stone necklaces, a hoe and a variety of flint implements (a dagger and triangular-based arrow heads) were retrieved from the deepest layer (layer IV). A large number of objects from a new phase of occupation (VNSP I Horizon) were located in the third layer and, lastly, objects from the Bell Beaker Culture and the Bronze Age were found in superior layers above fallen dry stone domes.

It can be deduced from the observations above that the Pai Mogo monument was constructed before the "Importation Horizon" of the Chalcolithic Period.

On the other hand, if we take into account C^{14} and TLM dates, as well as the analysis of cultural artefacts (round and oval-sectioned axe-heads, slate plaques, and the apparent absence of metal artefacts), we can conclude that tholos tombs already existed in the Alentejo as of the Late Neolithic Period.

The stratigrapy and the construction of the Comenda and Farisoa mounds indicate that the tholos tombs were constructed after the megalithic tombs, despite problems with the TLM dates, as shown by Whittle and Arnaud already in 1975.

The tholos tombs from the Upper Alentejo seem to begin with the Vale-de-Rodrigo site in which a typically megalithic infrastructure is superimposed on a dry stone corbelled vault. These conclusions are based on the following facts:

a) Its megalithic construction, similar to the large dolmens of the Megalithic Culture of the Alentejo.

b) Its location in a densely megalithic region and its proximity to the Escoural Cave (an important site for the understanding of the neolithisation process in the Upper Alentejo) and the Montemor-o-Novo Region, where a proto-dolmen nucleus appears to initiate the Megalithic Complex of the Alentejo, as has already been discussed.

c) Its funerary offerings, similar to those from passage-graves of the Alentejo: axe-heads, other polished implements and an important collection of engraved slate plaques.

Thus, links between Vale-de-Rodrigo and dolmens of the Alentejo are highly likely, without the need for a cultural break between the two kinds of construction. The appearance of a roughly corbelled roof over the megalithic chamber of Vale-de-Rodrigo ought to be understood as the result of specific architectural needs or even socio-cultural needs, and not foreign influences.

Furthermore, the Escoural tholos of fine stone slabs may be ascribed to the Neolithic Period; this new mode of construction implies a shift to a lighter structure in which nothing affects the stability of the dome covering because it is not supported by heavy orthostatic slabs but, rather, by the tumulus. Also, we should note that a large number of engraved slate plates have been found in the Escoural tholos, reinforcing the hypothesis that no cultural break occurred between entirely megalithic tombs and dry stone monuments.

A southward expansion of tholos tombs originated in the Upper Alentejo. Ten burials have been recorded in the Lower Alentejo of which eight have a fine stone infrastructure and grave goods linked to the local Megalithic Complex. Only the Cerro do Gatâo and A. dos Tassos tombs have dry-stone chambers, which could indicate contact with the necropolis of Alcalar where tholos tombs with stone slab infrastructures and dry stone walls coexist.

Although traditionally the tholoi of the Lower Alentejo and the Algarve have been assigned to the Chalcolithic Period, it seems plausible that these appeared during the transition between the Late Neolithic and the Chalcolithic Periods that peaked at the "Cupola Tombs Horizon", corresponding to the "Importation Horizon" of the Lisbon Region. On the other hand, since cultural parallels with the Southeastern peninsula exist, the author is convinced that dry stone circular chambers are forerunners to appearance in the Algarve of elements of the Millares Culture. In agreement with this, J.M. Arnaud elaborated in 1978 a three-part sequence of the Chalcolithic Period of the Algarve, placing the tholoi with stone infrastructure in an early phase and those of dry stone walls in a second phase. This new mode of construction, i.e. dry stone walling, appears in the Algarve as a result of a diffussion originating not in the Southeastern peninsula but in the Lisbon Region, probably arriving along the coast. This theory is based not only on architectural evidence, but also on the presence in Alcalar of varied archaeological materials typical of the Importation Horizon, such as limestone beakers and cylinders.

A metal offering from Alcalar 3 indicates that initial contacts with the Southeastern peninsula took place as late as the middle of the third millennium when tholos tombs of the Algarve were already in use. The Copper Age in the Southeast closes with the Ferradeira Horizon, between 2000 and 1800 BC, at a moment when collective burials begin to disappear, giving way to individual graves that demonstrate the primacy of the individual over the collective group in the Megalithic Period.

4. SUMMARY

Once we have finally overcome simplistic diffusionist and neodiffusionist theories, we must accept that several independent centres saw the origins of megaliths synchronically. Many questions remain, heavy as stoneslabs, sometimes becoming more complicated in the light of confusing approaches from funcionalist, processual, Marxist, postporcessual and other standpoints. It is possible, however, to attempt a summary of established knowledge.

a) The phenomenon seems to emerge from local social and economic dynamics in segmentary groups, where the collective tomb serves as a focal point for the definition of territories. C. Renfrew's 1976 theory remains plausible: the pression exerted on Atlantic Mesolithic communities, motivated by the expansion of farmer groups from East to West, would have stimulated the construction of cairns as landmarks and/or symbols of group solidarity. Besides marking the space, the megalith could have played a role in the materialis ation of rivality for the land: the ancestors' tomb would serve to institutionalise the possession of the territory from ancestral times. In this sense, the megalith would have a ritual role in strengthening social inequality or, as stated by R. Bradley, the monuments would be stimuli of economic processes.

b) In order to explain the origins of megaliths, the peculiarities of local environments and internal dynamics must be considered before resorting to external influences. The process would be interpreted as a part of the neolithic mode of production, directly related to sedentism and to new funerary conceptions leading to monumentality: the megalith would, at the same time, mark funerary, social and economic spaces.

c) On this basis, it is possible to explain the the vast monuments (Barnenez, Newgrange, Bougon, the large dolmens in the Alentejo, the necropolis of Alcalar – to name but a few) as products of a social and economic evolution that started in the early Neolithic, with societies which were probably not as egalitarian as once believed. As contended by G. Eogan for the Irish scenario, monuments such as those in the Boyne valley require prosperity, power organisation, egineering and ritual domination.

d) In the realm of mentalities, this is a religious phenomenon of great scope, of significance well beyond the simple burial and funerary ritual. The Megalithic Complex marks the beginning of the end of an egalitarian equilibrium, and the origins of elites.

The Atlantic megalithic phenomenon is such a complex, polimorfic, plural and and universal phenomenon, with continuities and differences recorded across a huge chronological and geographic area, that the brief synthesis attempted here may be suitably ended using C. Masset's words:

"This survey through the collective burials of Western Europe will surely leave the reader with an impression of complexity; this description is, however, oversimplified. We are dealing with a subject where humans have left their mark, where centuries are counted in dozens, over a million square kilometres. A certain degree of diversity was unavoidable."

Author's Address

Antón A. RODRÍGUEZ CASAL
Departamento de Historia I.
Universidade de Santiago de Compostela
Praza da Universidade, 1
15703 Santiago de Compostela. SPAIN
Email: phaarc@usc.es

Bibliography

BRADLEY, R. 2001. *The significance of Monuments. On the shaping of experience in Neolithic and Bronze Age Europe.* London.

BRIARD, J. 1995. *Les mégalithes de l'Europe Atlantique. Architecture et art funéraire (5000-2000 avant J.-C).* Paris.

CHAMBON, Ph., 2003. *Les morts dans les sépultures collectives néolithiques en France.* Paris.

DANIEL, G. 1958. *The Megalithic Builders of Western Europe.* Londres.

DARVILL, T. & MALONE, C. (eds.). 2003. *Megaliths from Antiquity.* Cambridge.

EBBESEN, K. 1985. *Fortidsminderegistrering i Danmark.* Copenhagen.

EOGAN, G. 1986. *Knowth and the Passage-Tombs of Ireland.* London.

GIOT, P.-R. 1995. *Bretagne des Mégalithes.* Rennes.

GONÇALVES, V., (dir.) 2000. *Muitas antas, pouca gente.* Lisboa.

GUILAINE, J. (ed.). 1998. *Sépultures d'Occident et Genèses des Megalithismes*. Paris.

GUILAINE, J. 1999. *Mégalithismes de l'Atlantique à l'Ethiopie*. Paris.

HARDING, J. 2003. *Henge Monuments of the British Isles*. London.

JOUSSAUME, R. 1985. *Des dolmens pour les morts. Les Mégalithismes à travers le monde*. Paris.

JOUSSAUME, R. 2003. *Les charpentiers de la pierre. Monuments mégalithiques dans le monde*. Paris.

LAPORTE, G. & LE ROUX, C.T. 2004. *Bâtisseurs du Néolithique. Mégalithismes de la France de l'Ouest*. Paris.

LE ROUX, C.T. (dir.) 1992. *Paysans et bâtisseurs. L'émergence du Néolithique atlantique et les origines du Mégalithisme*. Rennes.

LEISNER, G. & V., 1956, 1959, 1965. *Die Megalithgräber der Iberischen Halbinsel*. Berlin.

L'HELGOUAC'H, J., LE ROUX, C.-T. & LECORNEC, J. (dirs.) 1997. *Art et symboles du Mégalithisme européen*. Rennes.

MASSET, C. 1993. *Les dolmens. Sociétés néolithiques, pratiques funéraires: les sepultures collectives d'Europe occidentale*. Paris.

MOHEN, J.P. 1989. *Le monde des mégalithes*. Paris.

MOHEN, J.P. 2003. *Cultes et rituels mégalithiques. Les sociétés néolithiques de l'Europe du nord*. París.

OLIVEIRA JORGE, V. 1982. *Megalitismo do Norte de Portugal: o distrito do Porto. Os monumentos e a sua problemática no contexto europeo*. Porto.

RAMIL REGO, E. (ed.). 1996. *El fenómeno megalítico en Galicia*. Vilalba.

RENFREW, C. (ed.). 1983. *The Megalithic Monuments of Western Europe*. London.

ROCHE, H. et al. (eds.). 2004. *From megaliths to metals: essays in honour of George Eogan*. Oxford.

RODRÍGUEZ CASAL, A.A. (ed.). 1997. *O Neolítico atlántico e as orixes do megalitismo*. Santiago de Compostela.

RUSSELL, M. 2002. *Monuments of the Neolithic*. London.

SHEE TWOHIG, E. 1981. *The megalithic art of western Europe*. Oxford.

SHEE TWOHIG, E. 1990. *Irish Megalithic Tombs*. Risborough.

SCARRE, Ch. (ed.) 2002. *Monuments and Landscape in Atlantic Europe. Perception and Society during the Neolithic and Early Bronze Age*. London.

SOULIER, Ph. (dir.). 1998. *La France des dolmens et des sépultures collectives (4500-2000 avant J.-C.)*. Paris.

VV.AA. 1990. *Probleme der Megalithgräberforschung*. Walter de Gruyter. Berlin.

WOODWARD, A. 2002. *British barrows: a matter of life and death*. London.

THE MEGALITHIC COMPLEX IN CANTABRIAN SPAIN

Pablo ARIAS, Angel ARMENDARIZ & Luis C. TEIRA

Abstract: The present article describes the characteristics of the megalithic complex in Cantrabrian Spain. In this region, situated on the Atlantic coast in the north of Spain, more than 1250 monuments are known, including menhirs and above all megalithic tombs, distributed in a relatively uniform way across the area, from the coastline to the high interior mountains. The megalithic tombs are generally simple and small, although notable architectonic varieties exist. Some of them conserve examples of wall art. Radiocarbon dates suggest that most monuments have been built at the end of the 5th millennium cal BC and the first half of the 4th, whilst the grave goods that have been recovered inside them show a use of these monuments until the end of the Chalcolithic, in the 3rd millennium cal BC.

Résumé : Dans cet article on étude les caractéristiques du phénomène mégalithique dans la région cantabrique. Dans cette région, située dans l'aire atlantique du nord de l'Espagne, on connaissent plus de 1250 monuments –menhirs et, surtout, tombes mégalithiques-, distribués d'une façon relativement uniforme pour tout le territoire, depuis la côte jusqu'à les hautes montagnes de l'intérieur. Les tombes mégalithiques cantabriques sont simples et petits, quoique il y a des importantes variations architectoniques. Dans les parois de quelques monuments des représentations artistiques sont conservées. Les datations radiocarbones suggèrent que la plupart des monuments ont été érigés a la fin du 5ème millénaire cal BC et la première moitié du 4ème , tandis que les dépôts funéraires montrent qu'ils ont été utilisés jusqu'à la fin du Chalcolithique, dans le 3ème millénaire cal BC.

AREA OF STUDY[1]

Our study is centred on an area known to geographers as *Atlantic Spain* or *humid Iberia* (ARIJA 1972: 214), excluding the region of Galicia at its western end. It is an area rarely used as a unit of analysis in megalithic research, despite the consideration of a single unit given to it by environmental studies or by other fields of prehistoric research, such as that of the Upper Palaeolithic. We believe it is important to use this scale of analysis, in which we are not in any case pioneers (DE BLAS 1997), as we aim to correct the misleading divisions inherited from the history of research in this field (see below).

The region is in the form of a narrow strip, 400km long and between 35 and 60km wide, with a bioclimatic personality very different from that of the rest of the Iberian Peninsula. The peculiarity of its environment is the result of the interaction of geomorphological and climatic circumstances. Its southern limit is clearly defined by an important mountain chain, the Cordillera Cantábrica, running parallel to the coast, whose highest peaks, in the central-western sector, reach above 2500m above sea level. Towards the east, the relief of the mountains becomes less high, with gentler slopes, until they meet the Pyrenees. Between the sea and this natural barrier, a cross-section of the terrain reveals a high-energy relief, as the land rises an average of 2000m over distances of few kilometres. In contrast, the southern flank of the mountains has a gentler relief, with more open scenery, until the level of the Castilian meseta is reached at a height of about 800m. To the north of this natural divide, the oceanic air masses, full of humidity, and the sea as a regulator of temperature, produce a temperate, humid climate with short summers and mild winters. The mean annual precipitation is over 1000mm, and can reach 1700mm in certain places. The mean temperatures reach 18-22° in summer, and about 8 or 10° in winter (TERÁN & *al.* 1978: 171).

The combination of high-energy relief and abundant precipitation has created short, torrential river. Where they cross areas of softer lithology, their valleys develop in a south-north direction, following the steepest slopes and producing on their sides narrow mountain ridges orientated transversally to the main mountain chain, and decreasing in altitude as they approach the coastline. Where the lithology is more resistant, the profile of the valleys is conditioned by the morphostructures, producing more sinuous courses. In any case, the valleys are the main organisers of the geomorphological units (FROCHOSO 1986: 42).

In association with this environment, a dense vegetation cover has developed, contrasting with the environmental conditions to the south of the Cordillera. This consists of temperate woodlands, with mixed oakwoods at low altitudes and beechwoods in mountain areas, accompanied by a wide range of trees and shrubs. At present, this natural region includes territory belonging to the political-administrative divisions of Asturias, Cantabria (only the valleys draining to the north) and the Basque Country (Biscay and Guipúzcoa) and small parts of Lugo, León, Burgos, Álava and Navarre

HISTORY OF RESEARCH

As occurred in other parts of Europe, the presence of numerous megalithic monuments throughout the hills and valleys of the Cantabrian Region, often in prominent locations, did not go unnoticed by the people who lived in the same areas in historical times. Their existence was the cause of all kinds of myths and legends, some of which still survive today, among the members of an almost

---

[1] The present article makes use of data obtained through the project of the Programa Sectorial de Promoción del Conocimiento de la Dirección General de Enseñanza Superior e Investigación Científica "La transición al Neolítico en la región Cantábrica. Cronología, subsistencia y organización social" (PB98-1098-C02).

extinguished traditional culture. Thus, their construction was attributed to giants, the "moors", demons, fairies, witches or other mythical beings. The interiors of the monuments were thought to hold rich treasures, accompanying the people who had been buried there in the distant past. The names that these monuments are sometimes known by are evidence of these traditional beliefs.

It is probable that these beliefs or perhaps the survival of certain preChristian rituals, justified, in the year 737, the building of a small church on top of the spectacular dolmen of the Capilla de Santa Cruz (Chapel of the Holy Cross), located on the outskirts of the Asturian town of Cangas de Onís. This building, politically linked to the birth and consolidation of the medieval kingdom of Asturias (of which Cangas de Onís was the first capital), provides the earliest recognition - even though it is in an indirect way - that we have of the existence of megalithic tombs in Cantabrian Spain.

As the megaliths are often very noticeable in the landscape, they were used in the Middle and Modern Ages as landmarks, signalling the boundaries between different towns or larger geographical areas. The first direct, written references to these monuments come precisely from those times. The now-disappeared mounds at Cal de Río formed part of the boundary of the medieval territory of Castropol (Asturias) according to documents of 1299 and 1313. Similarly, in the eastern part of the region, the province of Guipúzcoa, documents dated in 1495 and 1664 refer to ancient stone tombs (some would be interpreted as Roman in origin by the historian Gorosabel in 1853), used as boundary markers. More detailed descriptions were given by writers and travellers in the Modern Age, like Ambrosio de Morales and Luis Alfonso de Carballo (16th Century and early 17th Century), and in the Enlightenment such as Gaspar Melchor de Jovellanos, at the end of the 18th Century.

Nevertheless, it is only in the 19th Century that a real interest is generated in the megalithic monuments of the Cantabrian region, leading to their scientific recognition. The vague information existing before then is transformed into precise references, thanks to the fieldwork of amateurs and scholars, who fitted their observations within the *Celtomania* that was predominant at the time. Thus, iIn 1857, M. Assas explored the above-mentioned dolmen of Santa Cruz, describing and interpreting it correctly for the first time. The same monument was studied by Rada and Delgado in 1871, and by the Count of la Vega de Sella in 1891, although its paintings and engravings were not discovered until 1915, by J. Cabré. Around 1878, F. Soto Posada and the antiquarian R. Frasinelli emptied the chamber of the dolmen of Abamia, also in the valley of the River Sella.

In Cantabria, there are few references to megalithic monuments at this time, and these generally refer to the so-called dolmen of Abra (in fact a natural rock formation, and besides, south of the Cantabrian region), mentioned for the first time by A. de los Ríos in 1857. Until the middle of the 20th Century this "monument" is often referred to, as the only one known in Cantabria.

The situation was not much better in the Basque Country. Although in the valley of the River Ebro, draining to the Mediterranean, several dolmenic tombs were located and studied in the second half of the 19th Century, the same did not occur in the northern zone. The only research worthy of mention was carried out by the Navarran erudite J. Iturralde y Suit in the Sierra de Aralar, on the divide between the Cantabrian and the Mediterranean Seas, at the end of the century. However, it was precisely in this eastern part of the Cantabrian region where research into megaliths was to make the greatest progress in the second decade of the 20th Century, and where it has continued, with the forced break during the Spanish Civil War, until the present time.

In this area, and during the period before the war, the investigation was carried out by a team formed by T. de Aranzadi (anthropologist), E. de Eguren (naturalist) and J. M. de Barandiaran (prehistorian and ethnographer). Starting in 1917, together they discovered and excavated a large number of megalithic monuments in Guipúzcoa and Biscay. The results of this research, performed with the expeditious methods of the time, but with an early interdisciplinary perspective, were rigorous and regularly published in a series of scientific reports and a few brief general works (BARANDIARAN 1972-1984). This work allowed the first hypotheses to be proposed to explain megaliths and recent Prehistory in the Basque Country. In fact, those proposals were made by Catalan scholars, as, in the 1920s, P. Bosch-Gimpera, and above all his pupil L. Pericot conceived the existence of a so-called "Pyrenean culture", integrating all the megalithic structures in the Pyrenees, from the Mediterranean to the Atlantic (PERICOT 1925, 1950).

Meanwhile, research on megaliths in Asturias and especially in Cantabria fell behind considerably. In Asturias new monuments were discovered and documented. Thus, in the 1920s J. Fernández Menéndez excavated several mounds in Sierra Plana de Vidiago, and A. García Martínez, explored the important group of mounds in the Boal area. In Cantabria, this period from the 1920s onwards, was marked by the work of J. Carballo. His contribution is however limited to vague references to new megalithic monuments, interpreted from an orientalist point of view.

The outbreak of the Spanish Civil War put an end to research throughout the whole of Cantabrian Spain, and this was not taken up again until the 1950s and 60s, in different ways in each of the sectors.

The revitalisation of research into megaliths in these decades was again most noticeable in the eastern part of the Cantabrian region. The fieldwork of different prehistorians was accompanied by the publication of two important books. One of these, by J. M. de BARANDIARAN (1953), is a synthesis of the Prehistory of the Basque Country, giving a great deal of attention to megaliths, while the other, written by J. ELOSEGUI (1953) is an exhaustive inventory cataloguing all the monuments known in the area at that time. They were followed by another publication, by J. MALUQUER (1964), covering his own research on megaliths in Navarre. In the same years new work was carried out in Asturias, above all by the Galician archaeologist F. Bouza Brey.

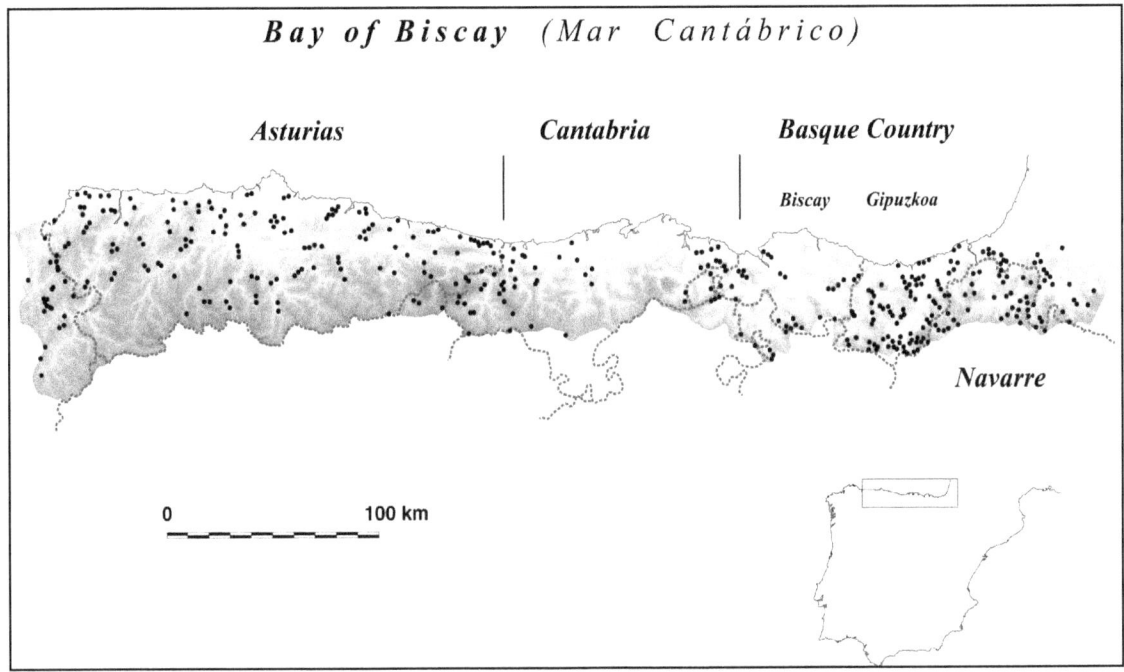

Figure 1. Distribution of megalithic structures in Cantabrian Spain.

In the 1970s, research continued fairly intensively in Asturias and the Basque Country. In the first of these areas, F. Jordá balanced his studies on the Palaeolithic with others on different dolmens and mounds. The first inventory of megalithic monuments in Asturias was published at that time; a catalogue produced with enormous effort by J. M. GONZÁLEZ (1973), mostly reflecting his own fieldwork, and which showed the wide distribution of these monuments in the whole of the area. In the Basque Country, the work of J. Altuna and J. M. Apellániz was notable, and culminated with the publication of the doctoral thesis of the latter, which despite certain interpretations that are now superseded, includes a complete *corpus* of megalithic monuments and their respective grave goods that is still of great use today (APELLÁNIZ 1973, 1975).

At this late time, only Cantabria remained as practically virgin territory from the point of view of the distribution of megalithic monuments. Although a few discoveries were made in the east of the region, this was only as a result of the expansion towards the west of Basque researchers. This inexplicable gap in the central part of the Cantabrian region was in clear contrast with the situation in the neighbouring areas to the east and west: the Basque Country and the Asturian-Galician area.

It can be said that the real increase in research into megaliths in Cantabria began in the following decade, and has continued to develop to the present time, basically due to the work of a new generation of archaeologists. In this way, from the 1980s onwards, a series of discoveries were made, permitting the publication, a few years later, of a book compiling an inventory with over a hundred megalithic tombs and menhirs (TEIRA 1994). The gap mentioned above was therefore filled, and the Cantabrian region began to show a relatively uniform density of monuments. These are years of intense activity, with the formation of teams carrying out archaeological excavations in the different parts of the region. The main contribution is the important program of research carried out by M. A. de Blas in Asturias since the end of the 1970s, both for his synthetic publications (DE BLAS 1983, 1997) and for the extensive fieldwork directed by this scholar in necropolis such as La Cobertoria, La Llaguna de Niévares and Monte Areo. Other studies that can be mentioned are those of P. Arias and C. Pérez in eastern Asturias, A. Díez Castillo, M. R. Serna, L. Teira and A. Armendariz in Cantabria, J. Gorrochategui and M. J. Yarritu in Biscay, and J. A. Mujika and A. Armendariz in Guipúzcoa. One result of this new stage of the research has been a large corpus of radiocarbon dates (see the appendix) and the publication of a wide range of papers (excavation reports, regional archaeological inventories, and general works) which have slowly contributed to understanding the scope of the megalithic complex in the region.

MOUNDS IN THE LANDSCAPE

About 1250 monuments have been catalogued in Cantabrian Spain. However, their geographical distribution is not homogeneous (fig. 1). While Asturias and the Atlantic part of the Basque Country have densities of about 7 monuments/100km^2, in Cantabria the density only reaches 3.44 structures/100 km^2.[2] The reasons for these

---

[2] 748 monuments have been catalogued in Asturias (10803 km^2 including the Cantabrian valleys of the province of León); 150 in the Atlantic part of Cantabria (4357 km^2) and 371 in the Cantabrian Basque Country (5270 km^2, including Biscay, Guipúzcoa and the Atlantic valleys of Burgos, Álava and Navarre). However, the actual number of monuments might be higher. For instance, in the archaeological survey that is currently being carried out in Asturias somewhat 500 new monuments have been found so far. Nevertheless the field work has been made by several archaeological teams, and it is not sure that they are always using the same criteria.

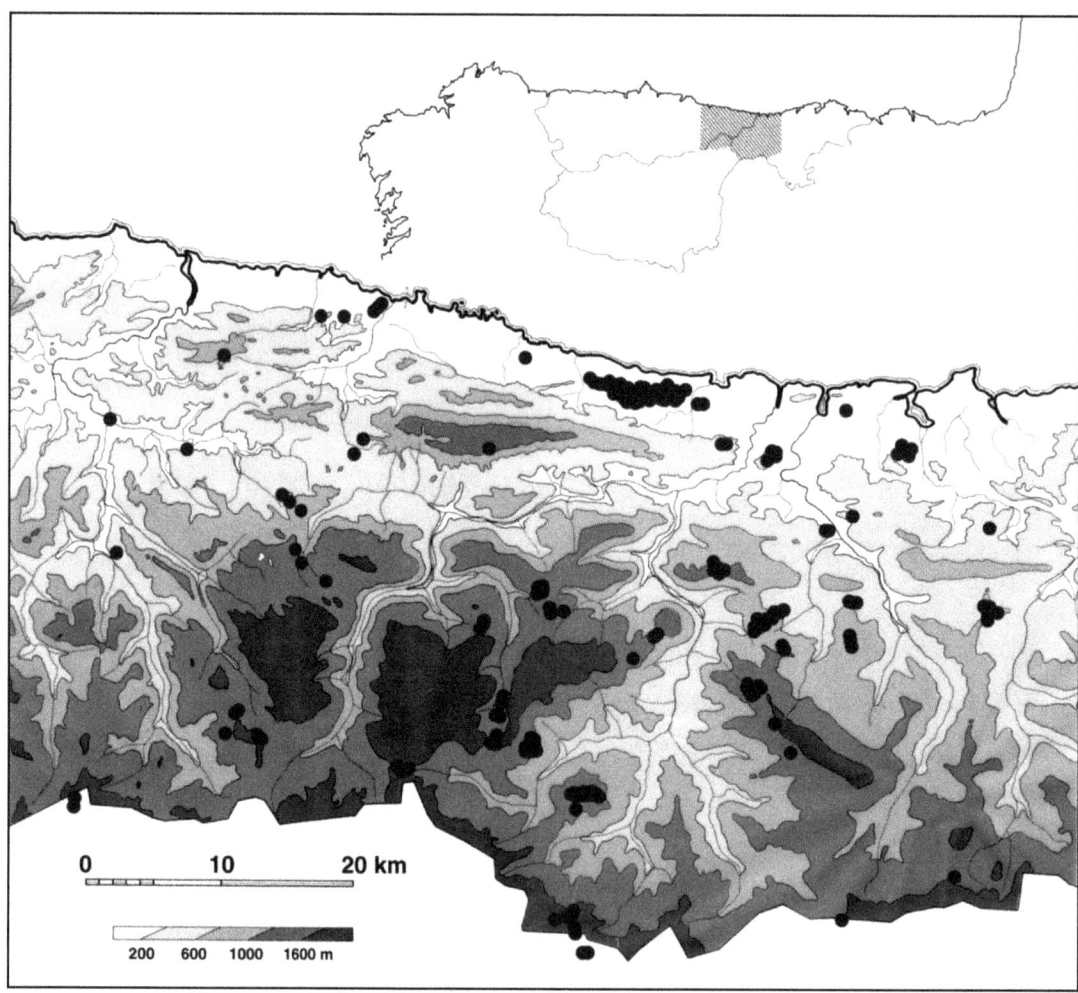

Figure 2. Distribution of megalithic structures in the area around the Picos de Europa massif (Asturias-Cantabria-León).

differences could lie in the behaviour of the Neolithic groups inhabiting the region, but factors derived from the less intense research in Cantabria are likely to be important too.

In the analysis of distribution models for megalithic monuments it is important to establish a correct synthetic description of the landscape in which the structures are located. In fact, the geographical interpretation acts as a parallel explanation, supporting the main archaeological reasoning. In Cantabrian Spain, the landscape is organised in a very different way from that of adjoining areas, like the Castilian Meseta and the head of the Ebro valley. In the same way, we should add that spatial studies in our area follow very different strategies from those applied in other parts of the Atlantic fringe of Europe, where the area is considered as a flat surface on which the monuments can be located with two variables, x and y. In the Cantabrian region, the third dimension (z) is necessary to understand the intentions of the builders of the megaliths.

The first characteristic in the distribution model for the Cantabrian is the tendency for the megaliths to be grouped (see, for instance, fig. 2). This attitude should be considered in a general way. On one hand, it is unusual to find positions with burial mounds from where it is not possible to see others. On the other hand, it is normal to locate several monuments, sharing the same personalised position in the landscape. What is the most noticeable characteristic of this landscape? Its energy of relief: the succession of valleys transversal to the coast in the middle part of their course, about 10 or 15km long. In the Basque Country the directions of the valleys are more intricate and chaotic. In Cantabria their long profiles order the dividing ridges from north to south. In Asturias we must distinguish between the environment near the Picos de Europa (with the greatest contrasts in altitude), the wide Nalón valley (which isolates a coastal area, separated from the greater altitudes in the interior valleys), and the western valleys (where the north/south rhythm of the central valleys is repeated). It is therefore a landscape that orders the biotopes and human land use in altitudinal levels. In this environment, megalithic monuments are distributed in positions dominating the surrounding area. This should not be taken in the specific sense of "see and be seen" from the exact location of each structure, but as a way of using a high position, special in itself. In those areas where the ridges form a narrow series of hills and cols, the megaliths are arranged in line along the ridge. In coastal areas, where the ridges are lower, with more open spaces, this behaviour is combined with the desire to overlook, in a selective way, low-lying areas. As an example, El Cotero de la Mina (San Vicente de la Barquera, Cantabria) avoids higher locations, making use of a small natural knoll in the centre of the valley to build a monument apparently almost 4m high, when in fact humans only added 1m to the original height. It is, furthermore, a structure with quite unusual architectonic characteristics. In this case, its unusualness is a result of the monument itself. The position of the grandiose dolmen of Santa Cruz (Cangas de Onís, Asturias) can be described in a similar way (DE BLAS, 1997a: 78). Both examples seem to define pieces of aggregation, linking with other smaller structures, placed in higher locations in the same landscape unit. However, in the area of Monte Areo (Carreño, Asturias), also on the coast but in more open scenery, over thirty structures of different typology are distributed in a dominant position in the landscape, constituting one of the most varied and interesting megalithic groups in the north of the Iberian Peninsula.

If we take this peculiarity of locating the megaliths in dominant positions as an established fact, the dispersion of megaliths in the Cantabrian region is evidence, in comparison with earlier periods, of the definitive conquest of the inland valleys to the highest altitudes. Monuments can be found from sea level to more than 1800m above sea level, with no altitudinal breaks in the examples. Megaliths can be found in each height group of one hundred metres. With these variations in the altitude of the dolmens, we can find examples in practically all kinds of biotopes, from grasslands to forests. So in this respect it is not possible to relate the locations of the megalithic tombs with any environment in particular, from which a specific economic use can be deduced. Therefore, the extreme cases of the highest locations make us think of alternative areas, with milder conditions during the winter, where it is more logical to locate the habitat or areas for the exploitation of resources.

The search for high locations dominating the landscape is not indifferent to the contrasts in relief offered by the different lithologies. A clear example can be seen in the mountains of the Picos de Europa, mostly formed by massive beds of limestone, and yet where three-quarters of over 200 megaliths are located on the intercalated siliceous rocks. The capricious forms produced by the erosion of the limestone, and the massive form of its outcrops, obviously makes it inappropriate for the building of structures which, it must not be forgotten, measure an average of 15m in diameter. It is also true that the areas on siliceous lithology are where soils and land suitable for economic use develop, and this may be related with the location of the megaliths. A third factor is connected with the relationship between beds of sandstone or quartzite and the position of the areas of communication, or passes, between the steeper and rockier areas of limestone. In this case, the linear distribution along mountain ridges is substituted by a nuclear organisation on these cols with less energy of relief. An interesting example of this kind of grouping is found at La Calvera (Camaleño, Cantabria) (DÍEZ CASTILLO, 1996: 93), with a dozen structures arranged on a surface no more than a hundred metres in diameter.

It is still difficult to evaluate the smaller number of monuments in the lowlands. Although some quite unusual examples are known, in general they are areas with a very low density of examples. The concentration of human populations in historical times may have contributed to the selective destruction of monuments. However, we tend to think that this difference in the density reflects the intentional behaviour of Neolithic inhabitants.

ARCHITECTONIC FORMS OF MEGALITHS IN CANTABRIAN SPAIN

When describing the megalithic structures in our area of study, one must choose between recurring to the main types used in classifications of European megaliths (simple dolmens, passage tombs, gallery graves...) which tend to "normalise" the sample, or make use of the lexis found in regional catalogues which, however, never contemplate Cantabrian Spain as a common space of reference. As explained above, the differences in the documentation between Asturias, Cantabria and the Basque Country, have caused separate explicative models. This fact creates a serious problem when comparing groups of monuments with clear similarities in form. As a consequence of these circumstances, we aim to offer an overall view, distinguishing between the characteristic and the circumstance, between the intention and the need, as both are useful to the study.

It must also be taken into account that the available sample is very unequal in this respect. The greater number of excavations in Asturias and the Basque Country means that much more detailed information is available for these areas than for Cantabria, where only about ten monuments have been excavated (ONTAÑÓN 2000).

With the information available at present, it is striking that there is an absence or great scarcity of some of the most common architectonic types in other parts of Europe, including the area surrounding the Cantabrian. In this way, no gallery graves are known, unless the tomb of Jentillarri E., (west Aralar, Guipúzcoa) is included in this type; it has a rectangular chamber of 3.9 x 1.2m, with an antechamber 1.5m long. Neither are there any mounds of the long barrow type, nor large cairns. The whole sample could be described as tumuli with a circular outer perimeter, without composite chambers or multiple tombs grouped under the same mound. In only one case, the dolmen of Pozobal (Ampuero, Cantabria) has it been argued that two chambers were below a single mound (SERNA 1997).

In the same way, no passage tombs, in the most orthodox sense of their definition, are known. The geographical distribution area of this architectonic type in the northwest of the peninsula has its eastern boundary in the valley of the River Navia, in the west of Asturias. This is the location of the dolmens of Entrerríos (Sierra de Carondio) or the mound number 6 in Sierra de Pumarín (Villanueva de Oscos) (DE BLAS 1983: 57). In the south the boundary of this type is on the southern side of the Cordillera, except in the dubious case of Igartza W (Guipúzcoa), on the divide between the Atlantic and Mediterranean river basins.

Therefore, the Cantabrian region is an area with the exclusive development of simple chambers and circular

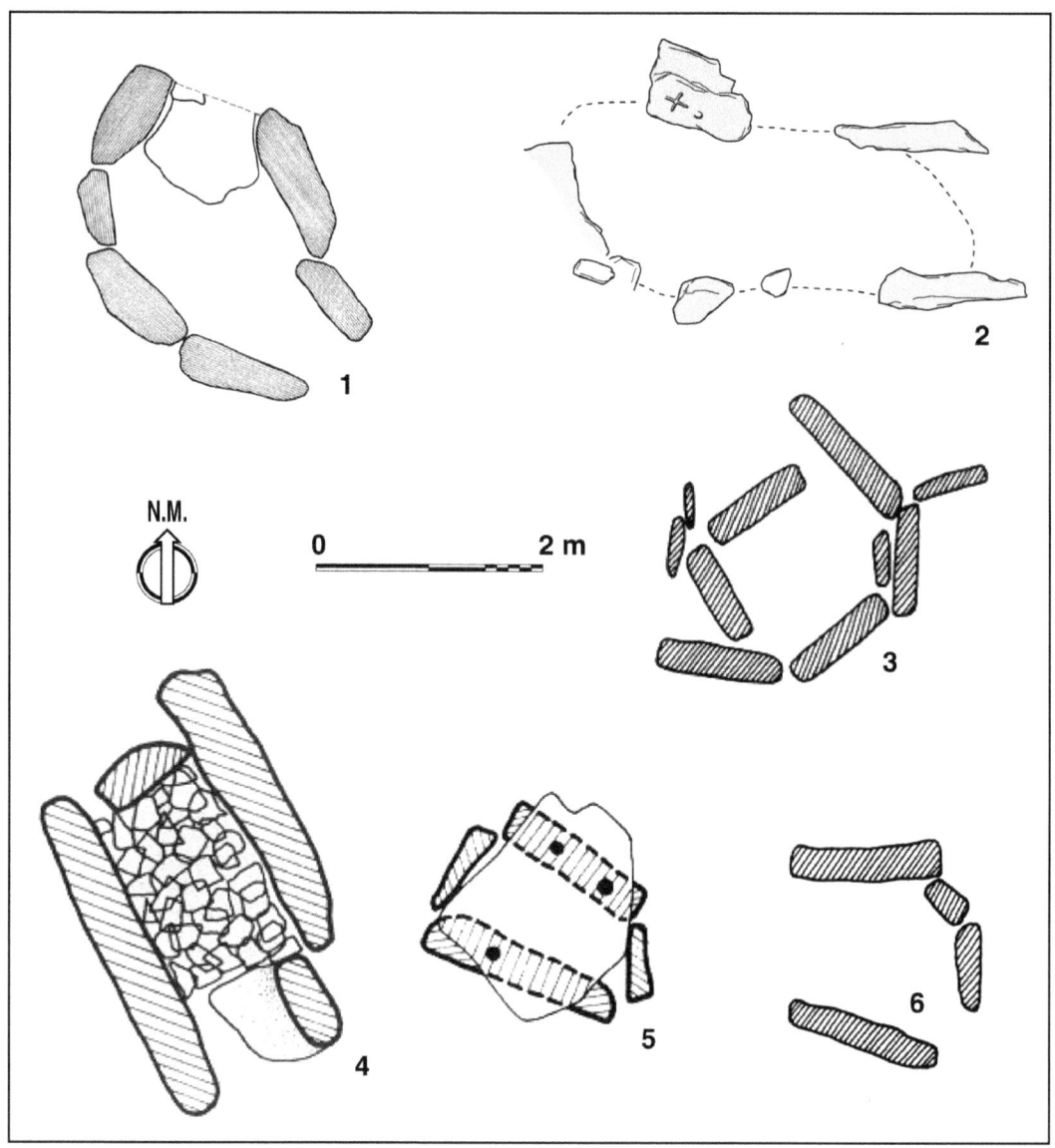

Figure 3. Examples of dolmen ground plans in Cantabrian Spain. Key: 1: Campa de San Juan (Salas, Asturias) (from DE BLAS 1983); 2: La Llosa (Cillorigo de Liébana, Cantabria); 3: Igaratza S. (Aralar-Enirio, Guipúzcoa); 4: Ausokoi (Abalcisqueta, Guipúzcoa) (from APELLANIZ 1973); 5: Aitzetako Txabola (Rentería, Guipúzcoa) (from APELLANIZ 1973); 6: Kalparmuñobarrena (Parzonería de Altzania, Guipúzcoa).

mounds. Within this apparent simplicity, however, we can find a wide variety of interior layouts, ranging from small spaces delimited by small flagstones, where it is not easy to imagine continued burial rites, to chambers 4 or 5m long with simple narrowings at their entrance as a kind of portal. At the same time, the outside of the mounds vary from mere piles of stones no more than 6m in diameter, to great masses of earth, or of stones and earth, conveniently intercalated to counteract thrusts or consolidate the surface of the structure. These can reach 35m in diameter and 4 or 5m in height. As will be seen below, there is no direct relation between the outer appearance of the tumulus, and the complexity or grandeur of its inner architecture.

In this respect, the conditions of the lithology on which the monuments were built should be taken into account. In most cases the construction materials came from the immediate surroundings of the monument. Only when the chosen place was close to a contact between two rock types is it usual to find a selection depending on the use of the materials in the architectonic structure. This is the case of Artzanburu (Oñate, Guipúzcoa) (APELLANIZ 1973: 224), a small dolmen whose chamber is made with limestone blocks, except its capstone, which is of sandstone. Or Jentillarri E (Aralar-Enirio, Guipúzcoa) (APELLANIZ 1973: 249), built on limestone, but with slabs of both limestone and sandstone, from a nearby outcrop, in its chamber. Another example, situated between these two, is the group of Pandébano (Cabrales, Asturias) (ARIAS, PÉREZ & TEIRA 1995: 40). Although it is located on an open col with sandstone bedrock, limestone blocks were quarried and rolled downhill from nearby crags to build the chamber and the mound. A particularly interesting and unusual case is that of Santa Cruz (Cangas de Onís, Asturias) (DE BLAS 1979: 726), where the enormous mound was built with cobble stones from the river terrace on which the monument stands, whereas the orthostats come from quite distant outcrops (at

Figure 4. Dolmen at Sagastietako Lepoa (Guipúzcoa).

least 2 or 3 km). In this case, the stones were probably selected out of the need for large flat slabs which could be used for paintings.

The most common model of sepulchral chamber has a rectangular or trapezoidal form (fig. 3), with a surface area of little more than 2m² and a little over 1m in height. The short sides usually consist of a single orthostat, and the long sides have one or two stones. The capstone, when it has been found, is formed by a single slab. The orthostats are hardly dressed, as in most cases sandstone and quartzite are used with flat surfaces. In these cases the name of *cist* has been used, although some archaeologists prefer to restrict this term to more recent funerary practices than the megaliths, when chambers of the same morphology, but smaller in size, were not protected by large mounds. From that point of view, the use of the term for megalithic monuments is to indicate smaller chambers (about 2m³), and a way of access by lifting the cap or by using the gaps between the cap and the irregular-shaped supporting stones. These two characteristics would mark their difference from simple dolmens. Some of these monuments in the form of cists are Monte Areo VI (Carreño, Asturias), Cantos Huecos 2 (Guriezo, Cantabria), Landarbaso (Rentería, Guipúzcoa) and Sagastiegako Lepoa (Guipúzcoa) (fig. 4).

A second group of structures is made up by those which have a rectangular or polygonal shape, but with one open side, generally facing east (for instance, El Baradal in Asturias or Arrobigaña in Guipúzcoa). In any case the chambers are still very small compared with monuments in the rest of the north of the Iberian Peninsula, and of course, with examples from other parts of the Atlantic fringe of Europe.

Similar to these two groups of "simple dolmens", we find multiple derived examples, which are often unusual because of their size. The dolmen of Merillés (Tineo, Asturias) has a long side 9m long and a single capstone over 3 tons in weight, and the long chamber of La Llosa (Cillorigo de Liébana, Cantabria) has an ground plan of 3.9 x 1m (fig. 3.2). Other cases show small variations in their structure, such as paved floors, like at La Cabaña 2 (Carranza, Biscay) or Landarbaso (San Sebastián, Guipúzcoa), but with no specific characteristics differing them from the rest of the structures with a simple chamber.

Special mention should be made of a very small group of monuments that appear to have involved more careful construction, and which are unusual in several ways, not only in their form. The term of simple chamber is definitely too basic to describe them, yet neither can they be included in definitions that identify a separate funeral chamber and entrance passage. The most exceptional case of all is the dolmen of the Chapel of Santa Cruz (Cangas de Onís, Asturias) (VEGA DEL SELLA 1919), with a rectangular ground plan of 2.6 x 1.5m, facing ESE and open to the exterior on that side with a narrow opening in the form of a portal (fig. 9). The orthostats are placed with their long sides upright, so that a much greater volume is achieved although the surface area is not much larger than in the typical examples of rectangular or polygonal chambers. There is no doubt that the true uniqueness of this monument is the decoration of paintings and engravings inside, and which was the reason for a careful choice of stones (sandstone, limestone and quartzite), with suitable surfaces for decorating. It is also one of the few mounds with an elliptical perimeter, 37 x 18m in diameter[3] (VEGA DEL SELLA 1919). Similarly, it is also unusual in being located in the valley of the lower course of the River Sella, between high mountains.

The expression *dolmen with portal* or *vestibule* has also been used in the case of the monument of Monte Areo XV (Carreño, Asturias) (DE BLAS 1999: 31), a structure of similar size to Santa Cruz. It has the same number of orthostats, seven, all of quartzite, which are stood with their long sides upright. Here the entrance was indicated by

---

[3] It is possible that this unusual extended shape can be explained by alterations after its construction.

Figure 5. Portal dolmen of Monte Areo XV (Carreño, Asturias). Foto: M.A. de Blas.

Figure 6. Central structure under mound 24 in Sierra Plana de la Borbolla (Llanes, Asturias).

two stones that are lower in height than the other ones in the chamber (fig. 5).

The monument of Cotero de la Mina (San Vicente de la Barquera, Cantabria) could be included in the same group, despite the difficulties in its interpretation due to the poor state of conservation of the structure prior to its excavation. In this example the bases of two orthostats belonging to the north side of the chamber remained *in situ*. They were 5m apart, and in both cases they were stones that had been stood on end. In other words, it can be assumed that the inner chamber has a much greater volume than the simple dolmens in the same area. It is equally in a low position within the surrounding landscape, and as will

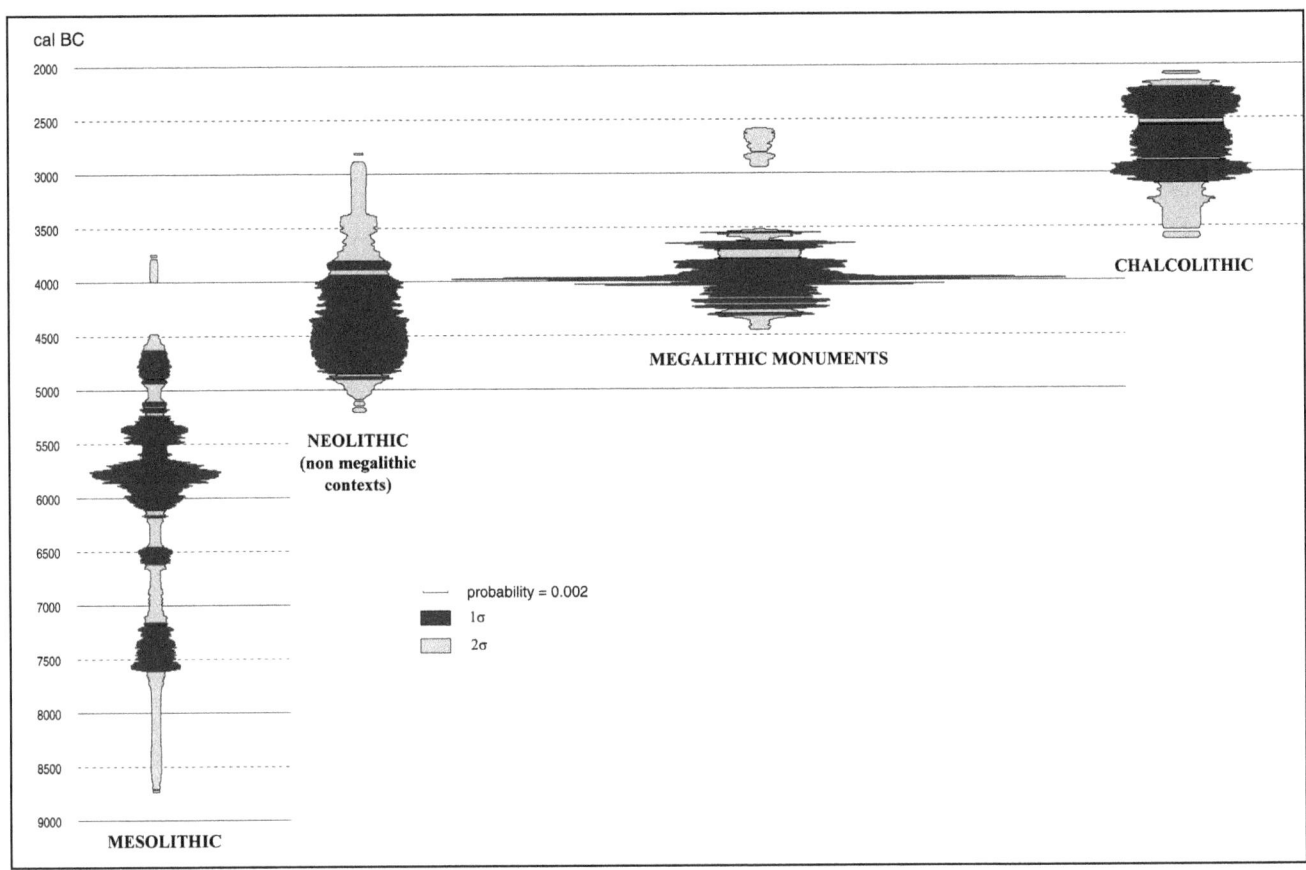

Figure 7. Probability distribution of radiocarbon dates in the Cantabrian region between the Mesolithic and the Chalcolithic.

be explained below, the large outer appearance was achieved with the minimum of work, by making use of a natural knoll.

Together with these large structures, other types of monuments have been studied without a conventional chamber, but with spaces defined by smaller stone slabs, pavements, wooden structures, simple holes dug in the ground, or even mounds without any kind of internal structure. The outer appearance of these monuments does not differ from the others nearby with more "orthodox" chambers; for instance the mounds A and D at Llaguna de Niévares (Villaviciosa, Asturias) (DE BLAS 1993: 167) are next to the monument C with a *normal* megalithic chamber. Similar characteristics are found in the mound number 24 at Sierra Plana de la Borbolla (Llanes, Asturias) (fig. 6) (ARIAS & PÉREZ 1990) or at Trikuaizti I (Beasain, Guipúzcoa) (MUJIKA & ARMENDARIZ 1991: 110). In the same way, the varied typology at Monte Areo (Carreño, Asturias) includes mounds such as Monte Areo V (DE BLAS 1999: 79), with simply an interior stone surface hidden by an earthen mound, which does not enclose any space apart from a post hole with the remains of a fire around it. The excavation at Monte Areo XII (DE BLAS 1999: 67), a monument 1600m to the southwest of the latter one, found something similar: a sand mound 24m in diameter covered several post holes. Two large oak logs lay on the ground near the holes, and the monument was interpreted as a wooden structure that had been burnt and destroyed before its burial under the mound.

SLOW PROGRESSION OR EXPLOSION? THE CHRONOLOGY PROBLEM

The considerable increase in research during the last fifteen years allows this problem to be approached with certain objectivity, due above all to the large number of radiocarbon dates, which have gone from five published in 1980 to the forty that are available today (see appendix). The distribution of the probabilities of these dates (fig. 7)[4] shows an atypical pattern, very different from the characteristic gaussian form of this type of sample (ARIAS 1999a). This suggests that the historical phenomena dated by these samples took place in a very short time. The distribution of probabilities indicates a commencement in the last third of the 5th millennium cal BC, an important concentration about 4000-3900 cal BC, and a rapid decrease in the 4th millennium.[5] The concentration of the probabilities for the dates of megaliths in the Cantabrian region in a few years around 4000 cal BC is reflected in the short duration of the *floruit* of this phenomena: 4082-3827 cal BC.[6] This information requires commenting on. In the first place, it does not seem compatible with the

---

[4] See ARIAS 1999a for details about that graphic.
[5] The chronology used in this paper is based on the calibration of radiocarbon dates by the curve INTCAL 98 (STUIVER & *al.* 1998). The calculations were made with the aid of the program CALIB version 4.3 (2000) (STUIVER & REIMER 1993).
[6] Following AITCHINSON, OTTAWAY & AL RUZAIZA (1991), *floruit* is understood as the period included within 50% of the probability around the median (between the first and third quartiles).

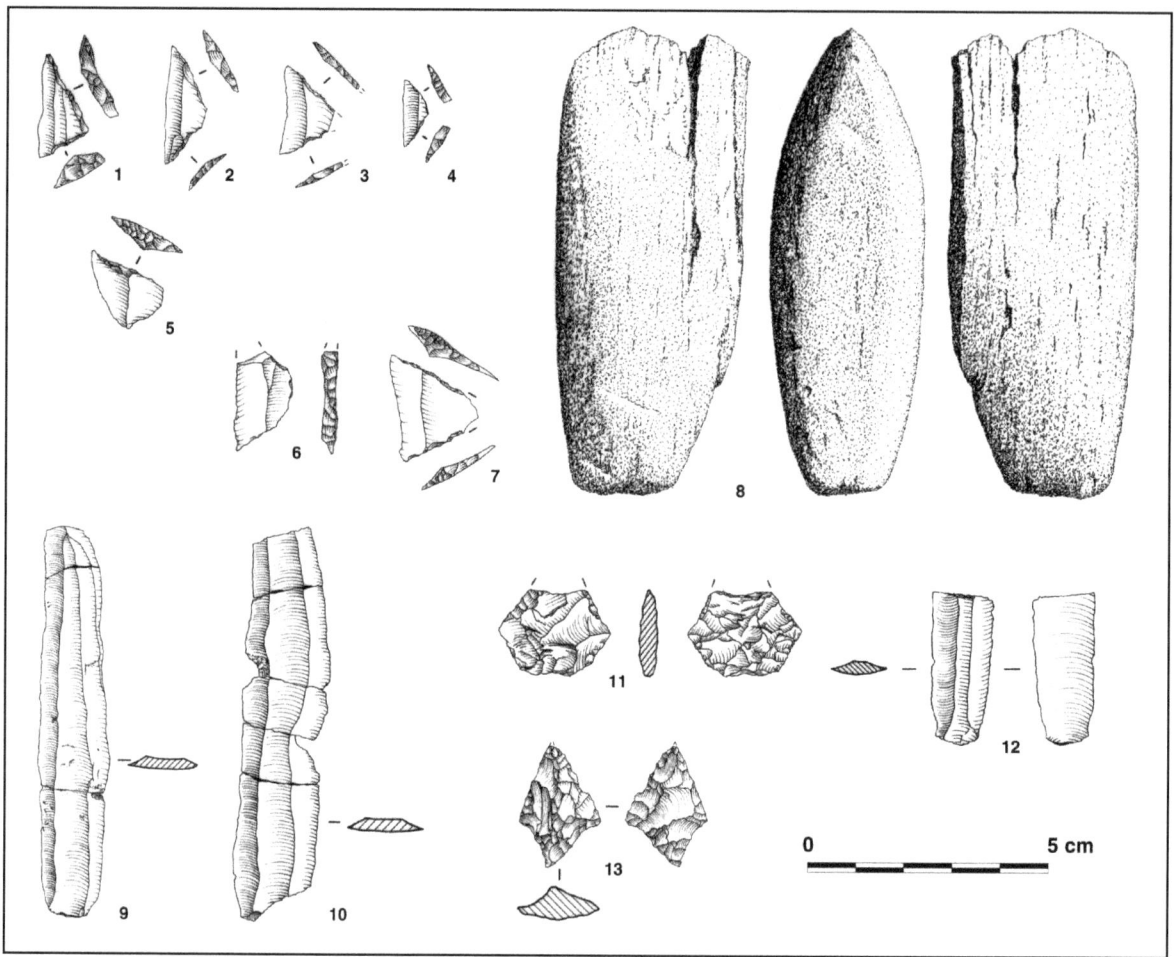

Figure 8. Lithic artefacts from megalithic structures in Cantabrian Spain. Key: 1-5: Alto de Lodos (Rasines, Cantabria); 6-8: Collado de Pelea (Cillorigo de Liébana, Cantabria); 9-10: La Raíz II (San Vicente de la Barquera, Cantabria); 11-12: Cires IX (Peñarrubia, Cantabria); 13: Vegabaño (Oseja de Sajambre, León).

hypotheses that could be made before knowing so many absolute dates. From the architectonic variability and, above all, the wide distribution in time of the grave goods (see below), it seemed reasonable to propose that the building of megalithic monuments had taken place over a long period of time, from the Neolithic to the start of the Bronze Age.

The analysis of this apparent contradiction is complex, as the evaluation of a group of radiocarbon dates is never an easy task. But in the case of monumental constructions, with presumably a long history, as is the case of megalithic structures, it becomes particularly complicated. It is necessary to determine, in each case, what exactly has been dated, or to put it in other words, what is the radiocarbon event (VAN STRYDONK & al. 1999) that has been dated, and what is its relation with the human event that we want to date, with the history of the monument. Unfortunately the excavation reports do not always provide sufficiently detailed information about these circumstances. In recent years, radiocarbon dating of monuments has become a routinary practice in megalithic research, but a critical exposition of what is being dated, and why, is often lacking. In any case, the available information can give some clues in order to tackle the problem described above. An important percentage of the dates of known source come from the palaeosoils on which the monument was built. This is because of several reasons, especially the common occurrence of charcoal in these soils, the ease in establishing their origin and, last but not least, the archaeologists' interest in dating the building of the monument. On the other hand, few samples date directly the buried human remains or structures sealing the chambers, probably owing to the poor conservation of this kind of material.

However, whether it is a strategy or an imposition of the monuments' state of conservation, the practice in Cantabrian archaeology for dating megaliths is not without its risks, as has been shown in other European regions (BOUJOT & CASSEN 1992). From a strict point of view, a date from a palaeosoil does not date the megalithic monument directly; it is only a *terminus post quem*, not necessarily immediately before the building. Therefore, it is not certain if the mentioned concentration of dates about 4000 cal BC really corresponds to a period of the massive construction of megalithic monuments or to another cause. Although the topic cannot be definitely solved at the moment, several reasons suggest that the answer is affirmative and that the charcoal in the palaeosoils does correspond to an event just before the construction of the monuments. First of all, the concentration of the dates; if the charcoal dated in the palaeosoils came from a sample taken at random of episodes before the building of the mounds, they would probably show greater dispersion in time. It is difficult to explain this concentration in time, unless there was some kind of generalised process of burning the scrubland, and its generalisation to monuments widely separated spatially is not easy. Secondly, in most of the palaeosoils analysed fully, horizon A has been in great part removed, so a greater separation in time between the charcoal and the monument would be expected, as the most recent deposit has been eliminated. Finally, the dates obtained in the last few years for structures clearly related with the building of the monument (Monte Areo), or apparently associated with it (Peña Oviedo), are similar to those from the palaeosoils. This suggests that the simplest explanation for the origin of the samples is that they come from processes of burning off the vegetation immediately before the building of the megalithic monuments, and probably related with it.

If this hypothesis can be confirmed (and the latest dates to be published are doing just that), some interesting conesquences can be drawn for the megaliths in the Cantabrian region. The most obvious is that the construction of the monuments was concentrated in a short period of time. The first megalithic monuments would have been built at an indeterminate moment in the last third of the 5th millennium, but a veritable "explosion" would have occurred about 4000-3900 BC. After this time, the intensity of the building would have decreased noticeably throughout the 4th millennium, and even more in the 3rd millennium, when there is hardly any evidence of the construction of new monuments. This means that in the Cantabrian region there was a great synchronic variability in architectonic types, as has been seen in many other parts of Europe (JORGE 1986, DELIBES 1995, BUENO 1994, to mention only examples for the Iberian Peninsula). Furthermore, there are no important differences in the dates for one or other of the sectors of the Cantabrian region, indicating a *grosso modo* simultaneous introduction of the custom of building megalithic monuments throughout the region (see below).

As mentioned above, the grave goods indicate a rather different panorama (see fig. 8). Although many megalithic monuments have provided materials coherent with a date at the end of the 5th millennium cal BC, or the first half of the 4th (geometric microliths, polished stone axes, long flint blades and even artefacts of Mesolithic tradition, like Asturian picks), it is quite common to find artefacts clearly datable in the 3rd millennium cal BC (arrow heads with flat retouch, bell beaker pottery, battle axes) and even some metal objects that could be attributed to the start of the 2nd millennium. This apparent contradiction between the grave goods and the radiocarbon dates must be resolved by the distinction between the building and the use of the mounds. The artefacts normally come from personal articles and funeral offerings accompanying the people buried in the tomb, and are therefore representative of the use of the monuments. This suggests, therefore, that Cantabrian Spain had been practically covered by megalithic monuments about 4000 cal BC, and that during the following two millennia the predominant practice would have been the use of these burial places, without excluding some continuity in building new monuments, particularly in the 4th millennium. In any case, this is a really notable example of the continued use of burial chambers, which needs to be explained fully. It is relatively easy to imagine the long duration in time of the use of really monumental constructions, like the dolmen of Dombate (ALONSO & BELLO 1995), but it is more difficult to understand the case of the more modest mounds in Cantabrian Spain.

RITUAL ASPECTS

The mental world of the Neolithic societies who built the megalithic monuments is almost completely unknown to us. In this respect, we cannot comprehend the monoliths or menhirs that are found, in relatively small numbers, throughout the Cantabrian region. Although some of them have been dug recently, the recovery of a few stone tools, and other artefacts, only proves their prehistoric age but throws no light on their possible use, which may or may not have been of a ritual nature. A little more can be said about the earthen mounds and dolmens. Their funerary character is out of the question, despite the fact that, in much of the region, the acidity of the soils has not permitted the conservation of bone remains. As a result, the next lines refer to these kinds of monuments.

The archaeological evidence available to us in order to understand the symbolic behaviour concealed in the construction of megalithic tombs comes from two closely related sources: the location and characteristics of the tombs themselves, and their contents, burials and grave goods.

The location of the tombs in mountain areas, often grouped together and forming a true necropolis, could be interpreted as an indication of the existence of "sacred" places, which in any case were not necessarily isolated from areas of everyday activity. Furthermore, the existence in general terms of a high degree of standardisation in the architecture - even with the relative variability that we have already described - is a sign of a series of construction guidelines or patterns, which ultimately must correspond to components of a religious nature. This normality finds its most rigid and clearest expression in the orientation of the open funeral chambers, which in the Cantabrian region (as in neighbouring regions of Galicia and the north of the Meseta) is directed systematically towards the east, and above all, to the south east, in other words towards the position of the rising sun in winter. Logically, in closed chambers, only an east-west or southeast-northwest axis can be identified. In consequence, it could be supposed that the tombs were usually built in the winter, if it were not for the fact that the high altitude of many of them makes this hypothesis impractical. In any case, their alignment towards sunrise suggests some kind of astral cult and possibly a symbolic association with death and rebirth, widely known in historical cultures.

Other structural aspects of megalithic tombs in the region can be interpreted as signs of ritual manifestations or activities. This is the case of some elements that are

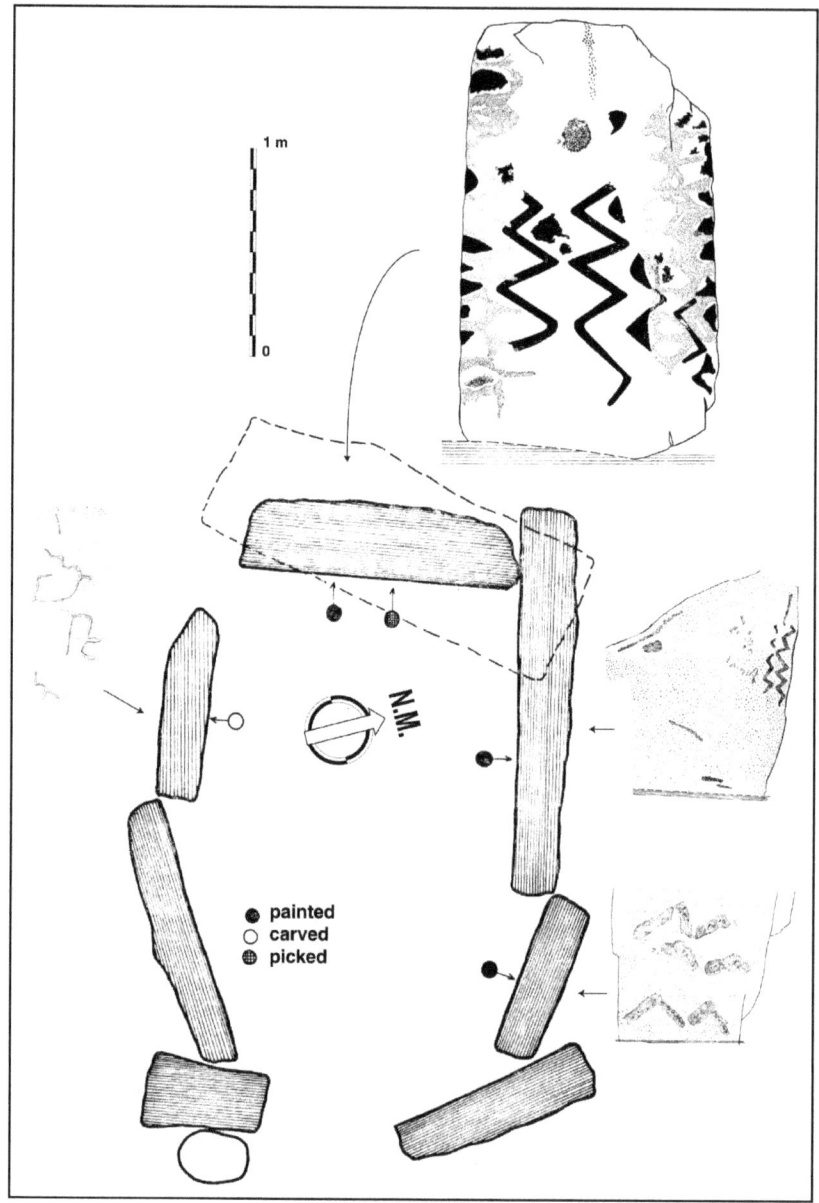

Figure 9. Distribution of wall art in the dolmen at Santa Cruz (Cangas de Onís, Asturias), after DE BLAS 1979.

difficult to explain from a merely functional point of view. An example of this, discovered in the dig at the recent Asturian monument at Los Fitos, consists of a platform or pavement built as a kind of appendix to the tomb; some thirty metres away a stone semicircle was found, in whose geometrical centre a fire had been lit (DE BLAS 1990). Many essential aspects linked to the sepulchral rituals have been lost for ever, such as the funerals and mourning, but structures like the ones described above suggest that there were complex ceremonies. The signs of fire, like hearths and layers of charcoal, seen in other Asturian and Basque monuments can probably be interpreted in a similar way.

But without doubt, the most obvious evidence of rituals is the existence of artistic works inside the chamber of some dolmenic tombs. The examples of decoration with paintings and engravings are limited in their distribution to the western sector of Cantabrian Spain, like an appendix of the much richer group in the northwest of the Peninsula. The boundary of the distribution of megalithic art is found in the east of Asturias (the valley of the River Sella), and can perhaps be interpreted as a boundary between different cultural traditions. Anyway, there are very few decorated monuments in the Cantabrian region.

The dolmen of Santa Cruz (Cangas de Onís, Asturias) is the best-known example and the most outstanding for the quality and profusion of its art (DE BLAS 1979). The uniqueness of this tomb is shown, as has already been said, by its atypical position on the valley floor and by its architectonic monumentality. Its chamber, which was emptied in ancient times, has four orthostats, out of the seven that form its perimeter, decorated with paintings and engravings (fig. 9). The most important group is located on the headstone, that was carefully dressed and smoothed, with a pattern made up of triangles and vertical lines in a zigzag, produced by a combination of picking the rock and red paint. Another two stones have similar lines painted in red, while the fourth has several non-figurative engravings difficult to interpret and some cupmarks. Originally other monuments in the region may have been painted, but if that is so the general destruction of the chambers and the effects of weathering have not allowed them to be preserved. Only in the dolmen, also in Asturias, of Penausén I, partially demolished and without a capstone, has a diffuse red pigmentation been recognised on two of its stones (DE BLAS 1983).

However, another two decorated stone slabs are known. These were removed from two Asturian monuments in the past, and are now deposited in the Museo Arqueológico Nacional (Madrid) and the Museo Arqueológico de Asturias (Oviedo) respectively. Traditionally interpreted as "stelae", their megalithic nature is now clear (DE BLAS 1994). The most notable, known as "stela of Allande", almost certainly came from the chamber of the dolmen called Tumba del Castellín. It is a large slab of worked slate, where incision and chipping have represented two series of concentric semicircles facing each other, and a sinuous or serpentiform figure. The image of a snake is a repeated motif in megalithic art (probably including the dotted lines found in the dolmen of Santa Cruz), and is interpreted as an expression of a complex mythology related with aspects such as life, death, renewal and fertility (BUENO & BALBÍN 1995) The other stone, known as "stela of Corao", is also a block taken from a megalithic monument, in this case the dolmen at Abamia (probably a covering slab). Its decoration is simpler, and reduced to a series of cupmarks, many of which are united by picked lines, forming an irregular and indecipherable design. Somewhat less complex examples of cupmarks, which we have already mentioned for the dolmen of Santa Cruz, are found in other monuments, general distributed in no particular order on the capstones. They are found in several Asturian sites, especially the dolmen at La Hucha, and also in Cantabria, particularly in the dolmen of Los Corros 2 (Vega de Liébana, Cantabria) (DÍEZ CASTILLO 1996).

Nevertheless, the Cantabrian region has some true examples of stelae. Two clear examples are known, found at opposite ends of the region, and yet with great similarities. They are two slabs that appear to have been worked to give them a trapezoidal, roughly anthropomorphic outline. The stela of Collá Cimera (La Cobertoria necropolis, Asturias), 1.4m in height, was standing several metres away from the dolmen, isolated and visible (DE BLAS 1997). The stela at Larrarte (Guipúzcoa) is somewhat smaller in size (0.56m), but very similar in appearance, was leaning inside the funeral chamber, among the burials, with a deposit of perforated stones at its feet (MUJIKA & ARMENDARIZ 1991). From the cultural point of view, both objects could be related with other stelae and more explicit "idols", located in monuments in the northwest of the Iberian Peninsula, such as Parxubeira and Dombate. Other unusual objects, in the form of "idols" should be mentioned too, like the painted cobblestone from El Baradal and the engraved stone from Las Paniciegas (although the context of the latter object is not too clear).

Human bones recovered in excavations at megalithic tombs do not give too much information. These remains come almost exclusively from monuments in the eastern end of the region, normally positioned on limestone hills, as the lithological conditions in the central and western parts of the Cantabrian region does not allow their conservation. The collective character of these tombs is clear, and they replace the individual burials in the Mesolithic, as found in several caves and rock-shelters of eastern Asturias (Los Azules, Molino de Gasparín and Los Canes). However, a tomb of an individual burial has been found in the cave of Marizulo (Guipúzcoa), corresponding to a time strictly contemporary with the megaliths. But even in those monuments containing human remains, the successive interventions in the site, combined with natural agents, have caused serious damage, fragmenting and dispersing the bones. We do not know, therefore, the way the bodies were deposited or even the number of them. Yet anthropological studies have shown the presence of persons of both sexes and all ages. In certain exceptional cases of good conservation, such as the dolmen at Larrarte, it has been shown that at least twelve people were buried in a chamber under $2m^2$ in surface area. A considerably larger passage tomb, Jentillarri, also in Guipúzcoa, contained at least 27 bodies, although the monument had been damaged and was not dug completely. In the nearby, small, South Igarratza mound more than 30 bodies were found. Equally, the dolmen at Larrarte shows evidence of a practice that must have been common, and which has also been seen in burial caves in the region (ARMENDARIZ 1990), consisting in reconditioning the tomb in order to leave space for new burials (MUJIKA & ARMENDARIZ 1991).

Finally, we must consider the grave goods, which also formed part of the ritual complex, and which usually accompanied the burials. They consist of very diverse types of artefacts, as corresponds to the presumably varied cultural traditions over such a wide area, and the long time period during which the megaliths were in use (see fig. 8). There is, however, a common background. An important part of this consists of certain stone tools that are standardised and apparently manufactured for the sole use of being deposited in a tomb. They are geometric microliths, mainly triangles and trapeziums, and flint blades of excellent quality, generally larger and better made than the materials in non-megalithic contexts. Together with these, polished stone axes and above all the arrow heads with bifacial flat retouch; first leaf-shaped or with small appendixes, and later, fully in the Chalcolithic period, with tang and barbs. These materials are usually accompanied by other, more ordinary stone tools, and even simple unretouched flakes and knapping debris. These may be found dispersed in the mounds or around them, and have sometimes been interpreted as vestiges of activities carried out before or during the building of the monuments and, therefore, with no ritual significance. The pottery is generally reduced to small fragments impossible to reconstruct. They are simple undecorated forms, although simple incised or impressed decoration has occasionally been found. Only at the eastern end of the Cantabrian region have some examples of bell beakers been found (fig. 10), of the cord-zoned variety of the maritime type

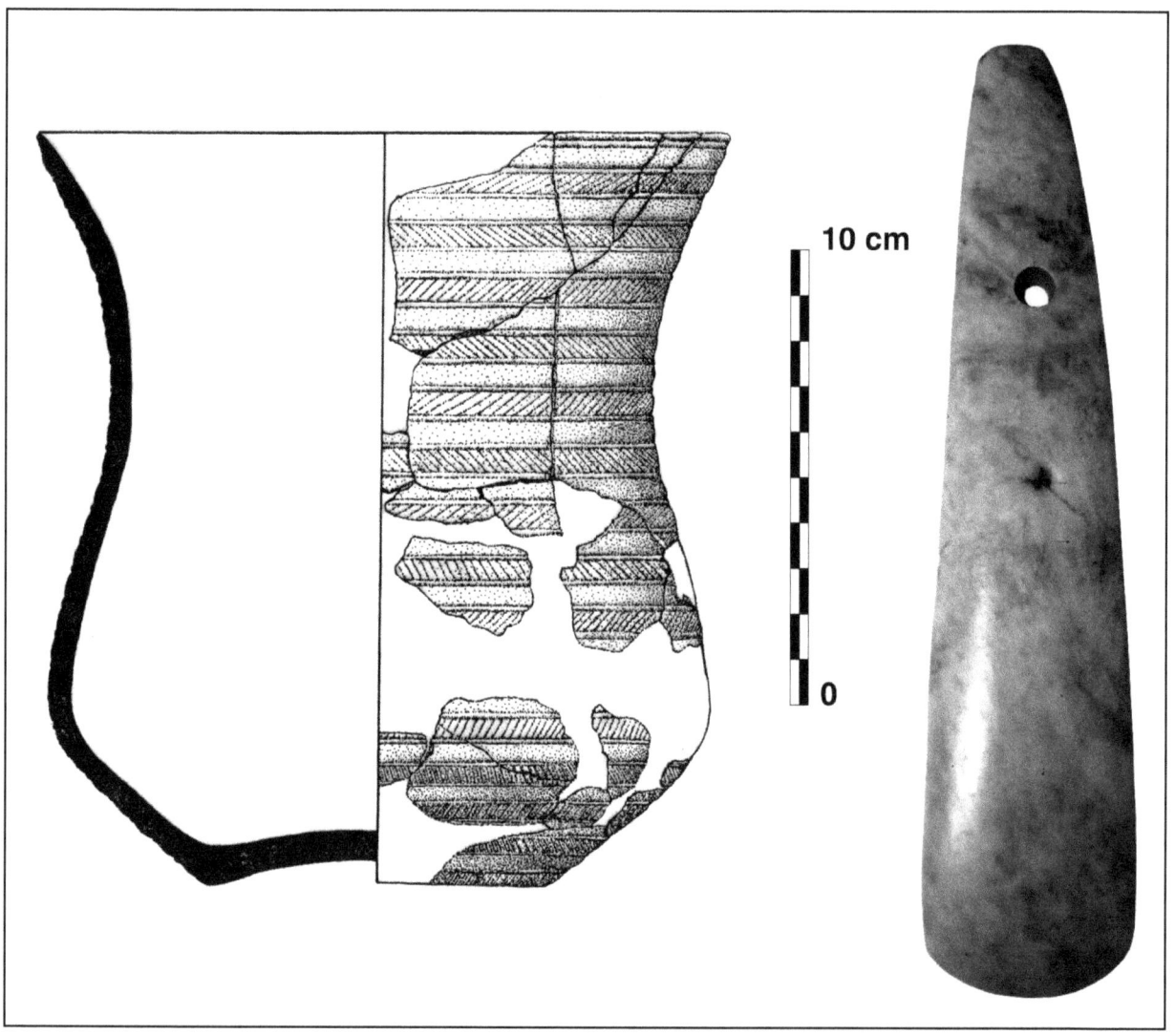

Figure 10. Prestige items from megalithic monuments in Cantabrian Spain. Bell Beaker from Pagobakoitza (Guipúzcoa) and perforated axe from the Dolmen of Santa Cruz (Cangas de Onís, Asturias).

(C/ZM) (HARRISON 1977). The objects of personal ornamentation are also frequent, mainly stone beads or pendants, including green stones of the variscite type, of lignite and even, very rarely, of amber, as well as other more recent objects like V-perforated buttons and wristguards. Together with all these objects, some very rare articles, as mentioned above, suggest contacts and relations with other areas of the megalithic culture.

SOME COMMENTS ON THE HISTORICAL SIGNIFICANCE OF CANTABRIAN METALITHS

The origin of megaliths in the Cantabrian region has not been the object of serious research until just a few years ago. In quite recent times, it was usual to recur to traditional "explanations" that defended without any reasoning beyond a supposed self-evidence of a supposed colonisation of the region by groups of animal-herders who, coming from other parts, brought with them as well as their flocks, the custom of burying their dead in megalithic monuments. However, no attempt had been made to propose explicit hypotheses that explain the problem and contrast them with the available archaeological information.

As we see it, three general scenarios can be proposed for the first megalithic tombs in the Cantabrian region, and on which more detailed hypotheses can be based: a) the megaliths are linked to the colonisation of the region by groups coming from outside, presumably from the neighbouring regions; b) the regional Mesolithic or Neolithic societies developed megaliths in a totally autonomous way; c) megaliths were adopted by Cantabrian populations as a consequence of their links with other groups on the Atlantic coast (through a process of acculturation, for instance).

The first of these scenarios seems highly improbable. There are no local precedents for any of the characteristic features of the megaliths (monumental size, collective burials), and nor are there any signs, as in other parts of Atlantic Europe, of phenomena which might justify its origin (development of social complexity, contacts with other societies). Besides, the chronology of the start of megalith construction in the Cantabrian region (similar to the rest of the Atlantic coast, but later than in some areas, such as Brittany or Portugal) does not support this theoretical line either.

The other two scenarios are worthy of more attention. In our opinion, the key factors to evaluate them are, on one hand, the comparison between the archaeological information provided by megalithic contexts and that of other contemporary or slightly earlier contexts in the region, and on the other hand, the chronology of the start of megalith construction in different parts of the region and the surrounding regions. The family of "invasionist" hypotheses would predict a great contrast with local tradition and a slow spread in time of the first dates for megaliths from the originating regions to the Cantabrian. "Autochtonist" hypotheses would be supported by the similarity between the megalithic contexts and the rest of the local Neolithic, and by older or contemporary dates in the Cantabrian region.

The little available data is not fully conclusive, but tend to support in a fairly clear way the second (and more complex) of the hypotheses families. The analysis made of the material culture of the regional Neolithic and Chalcolithic (ARIAS 1991, ONTAÑON 2002) show no significant differences between the megalithic and non-megalithic contexts, and the few that there are can be explained in terms of their function. Besides, evidence exists linking the earlier phases of megalith construction with the Mesolithic funeral tradition (see below). It must also be said, however, that some monuments of the beginning of the 4th millennium, such as the important group in the Sella valley, have grave goods and wall art suggesting links with Galicia and the north of Portugal (DE BLAS 1979, SHEE 1981), which could support an alternative hypothesis.

Nevertheless, in our opinion, the combination of the spatial distribution and chronology is decisive. The dates for the first megaliths in the region, as stated above, around 4300 cal BC, are distributed throughout the region, from Asturias to the Basque Country and, significantly, come from many of the monuments located well within the boundaries of the region, distant from the borders with Castile, Galicia and the Southwest of France, in many cases close to important centres of Mesolithic populations. Therefore, the available data indicates a simultaneous appearance of megaliths throughout the Cantabrian region, rather than an advance from one of its boundaries, as the invasionist hypothesis would claim. In this respect, it is also decisive to examine the situation in these supposed originating regions. The dates obtained in recent years in the surrounding areas are quite similar to those from the Cantabrian region. This is the case in Galicia and the north of Portugal, where the study of the distribution of probabilities in a very wide corpus of dates[7] concluded that there was no evidence that megalith construction started before 4300 cal BC, while the greatest concentration of monuments with simple chambers was dated, as in the Cantabrian region, at the start of the 4th millennium cal

BC[8] (ALONSO & BELLO 1997). The research of G. Delibes and his team in the north of Castile shows a similar situation, with an old phase, dated between 4300 and 4000 cal BC[9] (DELIBES, ROJO & REPRESA 1993, DELIBES & ROJO 1997). Neither is there any evidence that megalithic construction started before the end of the 5th millennium cal BC in the still quite poorly dated sites in the SW of France and the western Pyrenean area[10] (DEVIGNES 1997). Therefore, it is difficult to defend a classic diffusionist model for the origin of megaliths in the Cantabrian region. With the present data the most coherent hypotheses propose (and try to explain) that the first regional Neolithic societies, direct heirs of the local Mesolithic groups, adopted, at the same time as other societies along the Atlantic coastline of Europe, this assemblage of funeral uses, architecture and ideas that we know as the megalithic complex.

In this respect, it is particularly interesting to evaluate the relationship between the beginning of megalithic construction and the transition to the Neolithic, a topic which has been the cause of certain debate (GONZÁLEZ MORALES 1992, ARIAS 1997). From our point of view, the question has been examined from a too simple perspective (Neolithic = Megaliths, opposed to a Neolithic/Megalith sequence). In recent years it has been shown beyond any reasonable doubt that there are Neolithic contexts, with pottery and domestic species, several centuries before the building of the first megalithic monuments (ARIAS & al., 2000). However, in a region like Cantabrian Spain, the Neolithic transition should not be thought of as a single episode, but as a process of long duration. From this perspective, it is reasonable to consider that the introduction of the megaliths played quite an important role in the slow transformation towards Neolithic ways of life that Cantabrian societies passed through in the 5th millennium cal BC (ARIAS 1997). In fact, there is some evidence that the first megalithic monuments in the region developed in a Neolithic cultural context that still showed features relating it with the regional Mesolithic tradition[11] (ARIAS & FANO in press).

From this point of view, Cantabrian Spain is no exception. As one of us has previously stated, (ARIAS 1999b), the origins of the megalithic phenomenon along Atlantic Europe seem to be related to the social context of the transition to the Neolithic, if we understand it not only as an economic change but also as a process of transformation of both

---

[7] The sample studied by F. Alonso and J. M. Bello was of 72 dates from 31 monuments, after eliminating a few dates with serious problems of imprecision or of uncertain origin.

[8] It is interesting to highlight that the nearest chronologies to the Cantabrian are found in the north of Portugal, where the greatest concentration was between 4000 and 3800; in Galicia the concentration was somewhat later, between 3900 and 3700 cal BC.

[9] In the dolmens at La Lora, there are several older dates, from horizons A and B of the palaeosoils. But only one of these (from Valdemuriel 1, GrN-14128: 5670 ± 110 BP), around 4500 cal BC, is considered acceptable, with reserves, by the archaeologists responsible for the excavation.

[10] Hardly any absolute dates have been published. But the archaeological materials associated with the monuments seem to be mainly related with the middle Neolithic.

[11] As well as a certain spatial relation between the geographic distribution of the first megaliths and centres of Mesolithic population, we can point out the presence of objects often found in Mesolithic funerary contexts, like Asturian picks or long cobble stones, among the grave goods in megalithic tombs attributed to the end of the 5th millennium.

society and of the symbolic representation that society makes of the world. Megaliths might be, in some sense, a response to the tensions that the new ways of life would have produced in the indigenous communities. The megalithic tombs required considerable labour by many people and, by storing the bodies of ancestors, would help to maintain group cohesion. As A. SHERRATT (1990, 1995) has suggested, they could have contributed to the necessary readjustment of the social systems in the process of adapting to agricultural activity, as much in the economic sphere (collective work) as in the realm of ideas and shared values and sentiments (the attachment of the members of the community to a specific territory for example).

In this context, it is significant that polished axes, whose symbolic link with the new ways of life has often been stressed (BRADLEY 1998), become important in megalithic funeral deposits. Not only are they particularly common, but they include some of the clearest examples of prestige items in the early megalithic period in Cantabrian Spain, such as the long perforated axe from Santa Cruz (fig. 10).

From another point of view, the form of these axes is analogous with the production of other areas (the well-known Carnacean axes of the first megaliths in Brittany, certain Galician examples), apart from the fact that the raw material they are made of (fibrolite) is not found locally. In the same way, clear parallels exist between the paintings in the dolmen of Santa Cruz and those in the group in the northwest of the Peninsula (particularly the dolmen of Antelas, at Viseu, Beira) (BUENO & BALBÍN 1992). Therefore, it seems certain that this is evidence of social interactions and relations between the Neolithic communities in the Cantabrian region, and those of Atlantic Europe. This does not only occur in the early, Neolithic megalithic phase. On the contrary, among the grave goods of later periods, some exotic artefacts can be found, such as the gold ring from Mata'l Casare (Lena, Asturias), the perforated axe from Balenkaleku (Alsasua, Navarra), the gold and amber beads from Trikuaizti I (Guipúzcoa) and the corded bell beakers from Pagobakoitza (fig. 10), Gorostiaran, Trikuaizti I and Larrarte, all in Guipúzcoa.

Authors' Addresses

Pablo ARIAS
Angel ARMENDARIZ
Luis C. TEIRA
Departamento de Ciencias Históricas.
Universidad de Cantabria
Av. de los Castros s/n.
E-39005 Santander SPAIN
E-mail: pablo.arias@unican.es
E-mail: angel.armendariz@unican.es
E-mail: luis.teira@gestion.unican.es
http://grupos.unican.es/prehistoria

Bibliography

AITCHISON, T., OTTAWAY, B. & AL-RUZAIZA, A.S., 1991. Summarizing a group of ^{14}C dates on the historical time scale : with a worked example from the Late Neolithic of Bavaria. *Antiquity* 65, p. 108-116.

ALONSO MATHIAS, F. y BELLO DIÉGUEZ, J.M., 1995, Aportaciones del monumento de Dombate al megalitismo noroccidental. Dataciones de carbono 14 y su contexto arqueológico. In *1.º Congresso de Arqueologia Peninsular (Porto, 12-18 de Outubro de 1993). Actas*, edited by V.O. Jorge. Porto: Sociedade Portuguesa de Antropologia e Etnologia (*Trabalhos de Antropologia e Etnologia* XXXV, 3), vol. VII, p.153-181.

ALONSO MATHIAS, F. y BELLO DIÉGUEZ, J.M., 1997. Cronología y periodización del henómeno megalítico en Galicia a la luz de las dataciones por C^{14}. In *O Neolítico Atlántico e as orixes do megalitismo: Actas do Coloquio Internacional (Santiago de Compostela, 1-6 de abril de 1996)*, edited by A. Rodríguez Casal. Santiago de Compostela: Universidade de Santiago de Compostela, p. 507-520.

APELLÁNIZ, J.M., 1973, *Corpus de materiales de las culturas prehistóricas con cerámica de la población de cavernas del País Vasco meridional*. San Sebastián: Sociedad de Ciencias Aranzadi (*Munibe*, Suplemento 1).

APELLÁNIZ, J. M., 1975, *El Grupo de Santimamiñe durante la Prehistoria con cerámica*. San Sebastián: Sociedad de Ciencias Aranzadi (*Munibe* XXVII, 1-2)

ARIAS CABAL, P., 1991, *De cazadores a campesinos. La transición al neolítico en la región cantábrica*. Santander: Servicio de Publicaciones de la Universidad de Cantabria.

ARIAS CABAL, P., 1997, ¿Nacimiento o consolidación? El papel del fenómeno megalítico en los procesos de neolitización de la región Cantábrica. In *O Neolítico Atlántico e as orixes do megalitismo: Actas do Coloquio Internacional (Santiago de Compostela, 1-6 de abril de 1996)*, edited by A. Rodríguez Casal. Santiago de Compostela: Universidade de Santiago de Compostela, p. 371-389.

ARIAS CABAL, P., 1999a, Esquisse chronologique de la Préhistoire postpaléolithique de la région Cantabrique (Espagne). In *3ème Congrès International ^{14}C et Archéologie. Lyon 6-10 avril 1998*, edited by J. Evin, Ch. Oberlin, J.-P. Daugas and J.-F. Salles Rennes: Société Préhistorique Française (Mémoire XXVI) - Groupe des Méthodes Pluridisciplinaires Contribuant à l'Archéologie (G.M.P.C.A.) (*Revue d'Archéométrie*, Supplément), p. 259-263.

ARIAS CABAL, P., 1999b, The origins of the Neolithic along the Atlantic coast of continental Europe: a survey. *Journal of World Prehistory* 13/4, p. 403-464.

ARIAS CABAL, P., ALTUNA, J., ARMENDARIZ, A., GONZÁLEZ URQUIJO, J.E., IBÁÑEZ ESTÉVEZ, J.J., ONTAÑÓN, R. & ZAPATA, L. 2000. La transición al Neolítico en la región Cantábrica. Estado de la cuestión. In *3.º Congresso de Arqueologia Peninsular. Actas. Vol. III.. Neolitização e Megalitismo da Península Ibérica*, edited by P. Arias, P. Bueno, D. Cruz, J.X. Enríquez, J. de Oliveira and M.J. Sanches. Porto: ADECA, p. 115-133.

ARIAS CABAL, P. & FANO MARTÍNEZ, M.A., in press, Shell middens and megaliths: Mesolithic funerary contexts in Cantabrian Spain and their relation to the Neolithic. In *Stones and bones. Archaeological Conference in Honour of the Late Professor Michael J. O'Kelly. Sligo, 1-5 de mayo de 2002*. Oxford: British Archaeological Reports.

ARIAS CABAL, P. & PÉREZ SUÁREZ, P., 1990, Investigaciones prehistóricas en la Sierra Plana de La Borbolla (1979-1986). In *Excavaciones arqueológicas en Asturias 1983-86*. Oviedo: Servicio de Publicaciones del Principado de Asturias, p. 143-151.

ARIAS CABAL, P., PÉREZ, C. & TEIRA, L.C., 1995, Nuevas evidencias acerca del Megalitismo de la región de los Picos de Europa. *Férvedes* 2, p. 35-58.

ARIJA RIVARÉS, E., 1972. *Geografía de España*. Tomo I. Madrid: Espasa-Calpe.

ARMENDARIZ, A., 1990, Las cuevas sepulcrales en el País Vasco. *Munibe (Antropologia-Arkeologia)* 42, p. 153-160.

BARANDIARAN, J.M. DE, 1953. *El hombre prehistórico en el País Vasco*. Buenos Aires: Biblioteca de Cultura Vasca.

BARANDIARAN, J.M. DE, 1972-1984, *Obras Completas*. Bilbao: La Gran Enciclopedia Vasca.

BLAS CORTINA, M.A. DE, 1979, La decoración parietal del dolmen de la Santa Cruz (Cangas de Onís, Asturias), *Boletín del Instituto de Estudios Asturianos* 98, p. 717-757.

BLAS CORTINA, M.A. DE, 1983, *La Prehistoria reciente en Asturias*. Oviedo: Fundación Pública de Cuevas y Yacimientos Arqueológicos de Asturias.

BLAS CORTINA, M.A. DE, 1990, Excavaciones arqueológicas en la necrópolis megalítica de La Cobertoria (divisoria Lena-Quirós) y en los campos de túmulos de Piedrafita y el Llanu la Vara (Las Regueras). In *Excavaciones Arqueológicas en Asturias, 1983-86*, Oviedo: Principado de Asturias, p. 69-77.

BLAS CORTINA, M.A. DE, 1993, El Monte Areo, La Llaguna de Niévares y La Cobertoria: tres espacios funerarios para la comprensión del complejo cultural megalítico en el centro de Asturias. In *1º Congresso de Arqueologia Peninsular. (Porto, 12-18 de Outubro de 1993). Actas*, edited by V.O. Jorge. Porto: Sociedade Portuguesa de Antropologia e Etnologia (*Trabalhos de Antropologia e Etnologia* XXXIII, 3-4), vol. II, p.162-184.

BLAS CORTINA, M. A. DE, 1994, Las llamadas "estelas" de Corao y Allande: Su naturaleza y contexto megalíticos. In *Homenaje al Dr. Joaquín González Echegaray*, Madrid, Ministerio de Cultura (*Museo y Centro de Investigación de Altamira. Monografías* 17), p. 349-359.

BLAS CORTINA, M. A. DE, 1997a, El arte megalítico en el territorio cantábrico: Un fenómeno entre la nitidez y la ambigüedad. *III Coloquio Internacional de Arte Megalítico (A Coruña 1997), Brigantium* 10, p. 69-89.

BLAS CORTINA, M.A. DE, 1997b, Megalitos en la Región Cantábrica: una visión de conjunto. In *O Neolítico Atlántico e as orixes do megalitismo: Actas do Coloquio Internacional (Santiago de Compostela, 1-6 de abril de 1996)*, edited by A. Rodríguez Casal. Santiago de Compostela: Universidade de Santiago de Compostela, p. 311-334.

BLAS CORTINA, M.A. DE, 1999, *El Monte Areo, en Carreño (Asturias): un territorio funerario de los milenios V a III a. de J.C.* Candás: Ayuntamiento de Carreño.

BOUJOT, C. & CASSEN, S., 1992, Le développement des premières architectures funéraires monumentales en France occidentale. In *Paysans et bâtisseurs. L'emergence du Néolithique atlantique et les origines du megalitisme. Actes du 17ème Colloque interrégional sur le Néolithique, Vannes 28-31 de octobre 1990*, edited by Ch.-T Le Roux. Rennes: Association pour la diffusion des Recherches Archéologiques dans l'Ouest de la France (*Revue Archéologique de l'Ouest*, sup. Nº 5), p. 195-211.

BRADLEY, R., 1998, *The Passage of Arms. An archaeological analysis of prehistoric hoards and votive deposits*, 2nd edition, Oxford: Oxbow.

BUENO RAMÍREZ, P., 1994, La necrópolis de Santiago de Alcántara (Cáceres). Una hipótesis de interpretación para los sepulcros de pequeño tamaño del megalitismo peninsular, *Boletín del Seminario de Estudios de Arte y Arqueología* LX, p. 25-100.

BUENO, P. & BALBÍN, R. DE, 1992, L'art mégalithique dans la Péninsule Ibérique. Une vue d'ensemble. *L'Anthropologie* 96, p. 499-572.

BUENO, P. & BALBÍN, R. DE, 1995, La graphie du serpent dans la culture mégalithique péninsulaire. Représentations de plein air et représentations dolméniques. *L'Anthropologie* 99, p. 357-381.

DELIBES DE CASTRO, G., 1995, Ritos funerarios, demografía y estructura social entre las comunidades neolíticas de la Submeseta Norte. In *Arqueoloxía da Morte na Península Ibérica desde as Orixes ata o Medievo*, edited by R. Fábregas, F. Pérez, y C. Fernández. Xinzo de Limia: Excmo. Concello de Xinzo de Limia, p. 61-94.

DELIBES DE CASTRO, G. & ROJO GUERRA, M.A., 1997, C^{14} y secuencia megalítica en la Lora burgalesa: acotaciones a la problemática de las dataciones absolutas referentes a yacimientos dolménicos. In *O Neolítico Atlántico e as orixes do megalitismo: Actas do Coloquio Internacional (Santiago de Compostela, 1-6 de abril de 1996)*, edited by A. Rodríguez Casal. Santiago de Compostela: Universidade de Santiago de Compostela, p. 391-414.

DELIBES DE CASTRO, G., ROJO GUERRA, M.A. & REPRESA BERMEJO, J.I., 1993, *Dólmenes de La Lora. Burgos*. Valladolid: Junta de Castilla y León.

DEVIGNES, M, 1997. Quelques reflexionjs sur l'ancienneté du mégalithisme du Sud-Ouest de la France. In *O Neolítico Atlántico e as orixes do megalitismo: Actas do Coloquio Internacional (Santiago de Compostela, 1-6 de abril de 1996)*, edited by A. Rodríguez Casal. Santiago de Compostela: Universidade de Santiago de Compostela, p. 299-308.

DÍEZ CASTILLO, A., 1996, *Utilización de los recursos en la Marina y Montaña cantábricas: una prehistoria ecológica de los valles del Deva y Nansa*. Gernika: Agiri

ELOSEGUI, J., 1953, Catálogo dolménico del País Vasco. *Pirineos* 28/30.

FROCHOSO SÁNCHEZ, M., 1986, El medio físico. In:. C. González Sainz & M. González Morales, *La Prehistoria en Cantabria*. Santander: Tantín. p. 39-84.

GONZÁLEZ, J. M., 1973, Recuento de los túmulos sepulcrales megalíticos en Asturias. *Archivum* XXIII, p. 5-42.

GONZÁLEZ MORALES, M.R., 1992. Mesolíticos y megalíticos: la evidencia arqueológica de los cambios en las formas productivas en el paso al megalitismo en la costa cantábrica. In *Elefantes, ciervos y ovicaprinos. Economía y aprovechamiento del medio en la prehistoria de España y Portugal*, edited by J.A. Moure Romanillo. Santander: Servicio de Publicaciones de la Universidad de Cantabria, p. 185-202.

HARRISON, R.J., 1977. *The bell beaker cultures of Spain and Portugal*. Cambridge, MA: Peabody Museum of Archaeology and Ethnology, Harvard University.

JORGE, V.O., 1986, Polymorphisme des tumulus préhistoriques du Nord du Portugal: le cas d'Aboboreira, *Bulletin de la Société Préhistorique Française* 83, p. 177-182.

MALUQUER, J., 1964, *Notas sobre la cultura megalítica navarra*. Barcelona: Instituto de Arqueología y Prehistoria de la Universidad de Barcelona.

MUJIKA, J. A. & ARMENDARIZ, A., 1991, Excavaciones en la estación megalítica de Murumendi (Beasain, Gipuzkoa). *Munibe (Antropologia-Arkeologia)* 43, p. 105-165.

ONTAÑÓN PEREDO, R. (Coord.), 2000, *Actuaciones arqueológicas en Cantabria. 1984-1999*. Santander: Gobierno de Cantabria. Consejería de Cultura y Deporte.

ONTAÑÓN PEREDO, R., 2002. *Caminos hacia la complejidad. El Calcolítico en la región cantábrica*. Santander: Servicio de Publicaciones de la Universidad de Cantabria.

PERICOT, L., 1925, *La civilización megalítica catalana y la cultura pirenaica*. Barcelona.

PERICOT, L., 1950, *Los sepulcros megalíticos catalanes y la cultura pirenaica*. Barcelona: Consejo Superior de Investigaciones Científicas.

SERNA GONZÁLEZ M.R., 1997, Neolitización y megalitismo en la Cornisa Cantábrica: el yacimiento de Guriezo-Hayas. In: *II Congreso de Arqueología Peninsular*. Tomo II, edited by R. De Balbín Berhmann & P. Bueno Ramírez. Zamora: Fundación Rei Afonso Henriques. p. 199-206.

SHEE-TWOHIG, E., 1981, *The Megalithic Art of Western Europe*. Oxford: Clarendon Press.

SHERRATT, A., 1990, The genesis of megaliths: monumentality, ethnicity and social complexity in Neolithic north-west Europe. *World Archaeology* 22 (2), p. 147-167.

SHERRATT, A., 1995, Instruments of conversion? The role of megaliths in the Mesolithic/Neolithic transtion in North-West Europe. *Oxford Journal of Archaeology* 14 (3), p. 245-260.

STUIVER, M. & REIMER, P.J., 1993, Extended ^{14}C data base and revised CALIB 3.0 ^{14}C age calibration program, *Radiocarbon* 35, 1, P. 215-230.

STUIVER, M., REIMER, P.J., BARD, E., BECK, J.W., BURR, G.S., HUGHEN, K.A., KROMER, B., MCCORMAC, F.G., VAN DER PLICHT, J. & SPURK, M., 1998, INTCAL98 Radiocarbon age calibration, 24,000-0 cal BP. *Radiocarbon* 40/3, p. 1041-1083.

TEIRA MAYOLINI, L.G., 1994, *El megalitismo en Cantabria. Aproximación a una realidad arqueológica olvidada*. Santander: Servicio de Publicaciones de la Universidad de Cantabria.

TERÁN, M. DE & SOLÉ SABARIS, L., 1978, *Geografía General de España*. Vol. I. Barcelona: Ariel.

VAN STRYDONCK, M., NELSON, D.E., CROMBÉ, P., BRONK RAMSEY, C., SCOTT, E.M., VAN DER PLICHT, J. y HEDGES, R.E.M., 1999, What's in a ^{14}C date/Que'est ce qu'il y a dans une date ^{14}C. In *3ème Congrès International ^{14}C et Archéologie. Lyon 6-10 avril 1998*, edited by J. Evin, Ch. Oberlin, J.-P. Daugas and J.-F. Salles Rennes: Société Préhistorique Française (Mémoire XXVI)-Groupe des Méthodes Pluridisciplinaires Contribuant à l'Archéologie (G.M.P.C.A.) (*Revue d'Archéométrie*, Supplément), p. 433-448.

VEGA DEL SELLA, Conde de la, 1919, *El dolmen de la capilla de Santa Cruz (Asturias)*. Madrid: Comisión de Investigaciones Paleontológicas y Prehistóricas.

APPENDIX

RADIOCARBON DATES FOR THE MEGALITHIC STRUCTURES OF CANTABRIAN SPAIN[12]

Monument	Laboratory reference	Material	Determination (BP)	Calibration (cal BC) (after STUIVER & al 1998)	
				2σ range	Intersections
Monte Areo VI De Blas 1995: 101	GrN-19123	charcoal	5820 ± 70	4840-4500	4710 4700 4690
Monte Areo V	GrN-22026	charcoal	5470 ± 90	4490-4050	4340
Monte Areo V	GrN-22027	charcoal	5330 ± 50	4320-4000	4220 4190 4160 4120 4110 4060 4050
Monte Areo XII	UtC-7218	wood	5404 ± 41	4340-4050	4320 4300 4250
Monte Areo XII	UtC-7217	wood	5368 ± 44	4330-4050	4230 4180 4170
Monte Areo XII	UtC-7219	wood	5368 ± 42	4330-4050	4230 4180 4170
Monte Areo XII	UtC-7220	wood	5284 ± 42	4230-3990	4220 4200 4140 4130 4050
Monte Areo XII	CSIC-1379	wood	5261 ± 31	4220-3980	4040
Monte Areo XII	CSIC-1378	wood	5176 ± 30	4040-3950	3980
Monte Areo XII	CSIC-1380	wood	5133 ± 30	3990-3800	3960
Monte Areo XXII	UtC-7221	charcoal	4103 ± 43	2870-2500	2830 2820 2660 2650 2620 2610 2600
Mte. Areo XV	GrN-19724	charcoal	5040 ± 70	3970-3670	3890 3880 3800
Mte. Areo XV	GrN-22025	charcoal	4850 ± 40	3710-3530	3640
Larrarte	I-14781	charcoal	5810 ± 290	5320-4040	4690
Larrarte	I-14919	charcoal	5070 ± 140	4230-3540	3940 3880 3870 3860 3810
Boeriza 2	Ua-3228	charcoal	5500 ± 100	4540-4050	4340
Boeriza 2	Ua-3229	charcoal	5200 ± 75	4230-3800	3980
Hayas 1	GrN-21232	charcoal	5490 ± 120	4580-4000	4340
La Cabaña 2	Ua-3231	charcoal	5405 ± 65	4350-4050	4320 4300 4250
Trikuaizti I	I-14099	charcoal	5300 ± 140	4440-3790	4220 4200 4160 4150 4140 4130 4050
Igartza W	I-18214		5270 ± 100	4330-3810	4040
Sierra Plana de la Borbolla 24	OxA-6914	charcoal	5230 ± 50	4220-3960	4040 4020 4000
Peña Oviedo I	GrN-18782	charcoal	5195 ± 25	4040-3960	3980
Peña Oviedo	GrN-19048	charcoal	4820 ± 50	3700-3390	3640
La Llaguna A	GrN-18282		5175 ± 25	4040-3960	3980
La Llaguna A	GrN-18283		5140 ± 60	4210-3780	3960
La Llaguna D	GrN-1664	charcoal	5135 ± 40	4040-3800	3960
La Llaguna D	GrN-16648	charcoal	5110 ± 60	4040-3770	3960
La Xorenga	CSIC-1381	charcoal	5080 ± 30	3960-3800	3940 3860 3850 3840 3820
La Xorenga	CSIC-1382	charcoal	5059 ± 30	3950-3790	3910 3880 3800
Cotobasero 2	I-16442	charcoal	4960 ± 90	3960-3540	3710
Hirumugarrieta 2	Ua-???	charcoal	4955 ± 85	3960-3550	3710
Hirumugarrieta 2	Ua-???	charcoal	4865 ± 90	3920-3380	3650
Praalata	I-17195		4310 ± 110	3340-2620	2910
Sierra Plana de la Borbolla 24	OxA-6915	charcoal	3650 ± 55	2200-1830	2030 1990 1980
Piedrafita V	Ly-2939		3160 ± 130	1740-1050	1430
Piedrafita V	UGRA-191		2160 ± 110	410- AD 70	200 190 180
Bernalta 1	Ua-4251	charcoal	2905 ± 55	1290-920	1110 1100 1070 1060 1050
Bernalta 1	Ua-4252	charcoal	1495 ± 50	AD 440-650	AD 560 570 580 590 600
El Cantón I	CSIC-329	charcoal	2690 ± 50	970-790	830

---

[12] The dates posterior to 4000 BP, obviously corresponding to contamination or much later activities (for instance OxA-6916, which is related to a structure associated to the outer part of the monument) have not been included in figure 7. We have also eliminated some cases coming from paleosoils, when there are more reliable dates (thus, for Larrarte we have preferred I-14919 to I-14781).

LE PHENOMENE FUNERAIRE DANS LE PAYS BASQUE PENDANT LE NEOLITHIQUE ET L'AGE DES METAUX : CONTEXTES CULTURELS

J. FERNANDEZ ERASO & J.A. MUJIKA ALUSTIZA

Abstract: This paper focuses on the funerary world from the Neolithic to the early Age of Metals. The available information on the topic is updated and a systematic and holistic view of the phenomenon is presented, together with the economy and the ways of life.

Résumé : On étudie principalement le monde funéraire depuis le Néolithique à la première Age des Métaux. On mis a jour la information qui existe et se tâche d'offrir une vision globale et systématique de ce phénomène, la économie et les modes de vie.

1. INTRODUCTION

Le Pays Basque Méridional présente des zones géoclimatiques différentes. Le versant sud avec d'amples vallées a un climat méditerranéen bien qu'il varie suivant la latitude et l'altitude. Le versant nord a un relief compartimenté, avec des vallées étroites qui ont une difficile communication en direction est-ouest, avec des altitudes qui en un espace réduit montent de 100 a 600 mètres (du fond de la vallée a la cime), ce versant a un climat atlantique. Ceci donne lieu a une grande variété de biotopes, depuis les méditerranéens aux alpins, auxquels l'homme préhistorique doit s'adapter. C'est pour cela qu'il n'est pas possible d'établir un modèle de comportement commun à tout le territoire.

Pour cet article nous avons pris comme référence à peu près 50 gisements : dolmens, cavernes ou gouffres sépulcraux, endroits à plein air, etc.... Ces gisements ont été fouillés au cours des vingt dernières années et la plupart ont des dates C-14.

2. TYPOLOGIE DES GISEMENTS

Depuis les périodes les plus éloignées de la préhistoire, l'homme a cherché la protection des grottes et des abris sous roche, mais cela n'a signifié en aucun cas un dépeuplement des zones qui n'offraient pas de protection naturelle : l'homme fabriquait lui-même sa propre demeure à plein air. Dans le territoire dans lequel nous travaillons ces deux modalités de demeures co-existent. Au premier abord se sont les refuges naturels qui paraissent les plus appropriés pour servir de demeure. Pourtant ceci est une vision faussée vu que, étant donné le climat, les processus anthropiques, le relief compliqué, etc. la recherche a approfondi l'étude de ce type de gisements plutôt que d'autres. Ce n'est que ces dernières années que l'on travaille sur des endroits à plein air comme La Renke, La Hoya (Alava), Los Cascajos, Paternainbidea, Aparrea, Monte Aguilar (Navarre), tous situés dans la zone où il y a le moins de précipitation et où l'agriculture de type méditerranéen est très développée. Dans la zone plus humide, où les pâturages et les forêts occupent la quasi totalité du territoire, les gisements suivants ont été fouillés : Parekolanda (Epipaléolithique), Herriko Barra (Néolithique) et Haltz-erreka (Age du Bronze).

2.1. Typologie des lieux d'habitation

Dans le Pays Basque on trouve aussi bien des lieux d'habitation stable plus ou moins structurés, comme d'autres lieux à caractère provisionnel ou saisonnier de morphologie très simple, qui peuvent se regrouper en :

– gisements à plein air.

– gisements dans des refuges naturels.

2.1.1. Gisements à plein air

Dans ce type de gisements nous pouvons différencier deux systèmes d'occupation du territoire : l'un à caractère provisoire ou saisonnier construit avec des structures isolées, dispersées etc. et l'autre à caractère plus permanent ou stable formé par des groupements de structures plus solides, avec des fonctions plus diverses, etc.

Au premier système d'occupation correspondraient différentes concentrations de restes archéologiques dans des zones très localisées dans l'espace dont la fonction a pu être des fonds de cabanes, ou a pu correspondre à d'autres types de fonctions différentes (basse-cours, endroit de stockage, etc.) par exemples à La Renke, Herriko Barra, Haltz-Erreka, etc. On peut affirmer que certains de ces endroits avaient un caractère saisonnier et que leur occupation a été brève. Les restes matériels appartiennent en général au même moment culturel.

A l'autre système d'habitation, qui peut co-exister avec le premier, correspondent des concentrations à plein air de gisements composés d'abondantes structures de différentes caractéristiques (fonds de cabanes, silos, fosses d'enterrement, etc.) qui forment un village. Une des manifestations les plus vieilles et mieux documentée est constituée par des sites à fossés (Los Cascajos, etc.) qui semblent correspondre à des populations à économie mixte. Dans d'autres cas il existe des indices d'un habitat complexe, peut-être avec des structures un peu plus solides

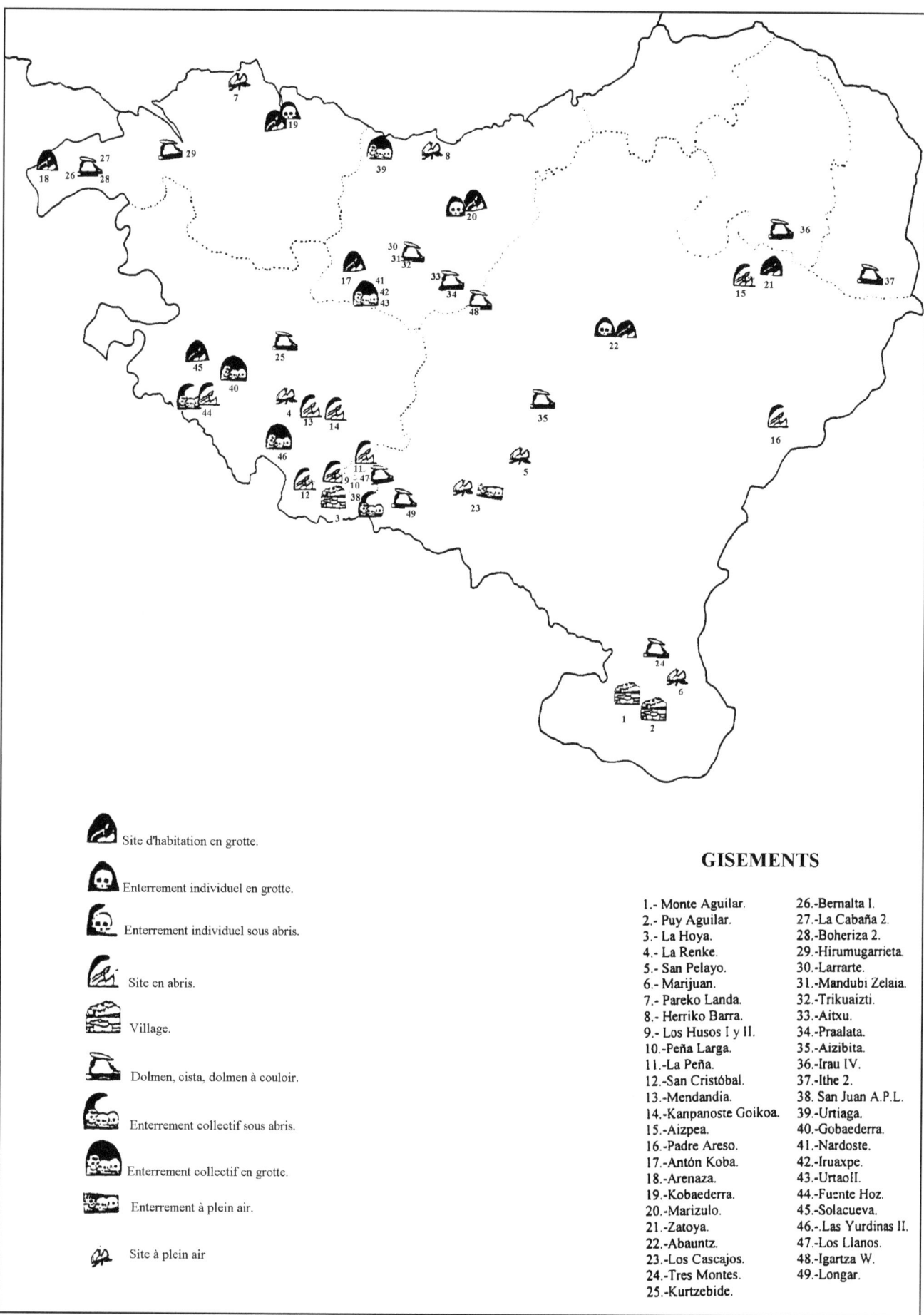

Figure 1. Carte de localisation des sites.

(Monte Aguilar, La Hoya, etc.) et une occupation plus étendue dans le temps, qui paraissent déterminer une occupation plus stable et permanente.

2.1.2. Gisements dans des refuges naturels

Parmi ceux-ci on peut signaler ceux qui se trouvent dans des abris sous roche et des grottes comme celles de Marizulo, Atxoste, Mendandia, Fuente Hoz, Los Husos, Peña Larga, Solacueva, etc. Ses endroits sont fréquemment utilisés ce qui donne lieu à une séquence culturelle longue et complexe, autant par ses fonctions que par sa chronologie. Quand il s'agit de grottes situées près du littoral les séquences stratigraphiques peuvent commencer dans le Paléolithique (Santimamiñe, Ermittia, Urtiaga, etc.) mais l'intensité de l'occupation diminue pendant le Holocène, ceci est sans doute dû a la création de villages à plein air. A ce moment les grottes souffrent un changement dans leur fonctionnalité donnant plus d'importance à l'utilisation sépulcrale, bien qu'il y ait des exemples d'occupation intense comme on le signale à Arenaza.

Dans le bassin du Haut Ebre il n'existe pratiquement pas vestiges antérieurs à la Epipaléolithique, bien qu'à partir de ce moment l'utilisation de ces refuges ressemble à celle des refuges de la côte de la même époque. Abauntz, Atxoste, Fuente Hoz, Mendandia, La Peña, etc. en sont des exemples. A une séquence culturelle qui commence bien au cours du Epipaléolithique (La Peña, Medandia, Atxoste : etc.) ou au Néolithique (Peña Larga, Los Husos I et II, etc.) se superposent des occupations Chalcolithiques de caractère funéraire, de refuges temporaires, d' étables, etc.

3. TYPOLOGIE DES ENTERREMENTS

Dans le Pays Basque nous avons pu détecter une série variée de types d'enterrements qui se produisent fréquemment dans les mêmes périodes culturelles et dans des chronologies très rapprochées, ce qui nous permet de déduire qu'il y a une co-existence de différents types d'enterrements plutôt qu'une succession de ces types associée à des périodes culturelles concrètes. Les types les plus connus sont :

1.- Enterrements dans :
    1a- des fosses à l'intérieur de grottes et dans des abris sous roche.
    1b- des trous dans des endroits à plein air.
2.- dépots en surface :
    2a- Sans aucune structure, à l'intérieur de grottes sépulcrales et d'abris.
    2b- Avec une structure construite à cet effet :
        2b.1- Cistes à l'intérieur de refuges naturels : Marizulo et Abauntz.
        2b:2- Dolmens et cistes à plein air.

1a.- Fosses à l'intérieur de grottes et dans des abris sous roche

Elles se conservent à l'intérieur de grottes ou dans des abris qui ont servis avant, après ou simultanément comme des endroits d'habitation permanente ou comme des refuges temporaires. Ils sont détectables, non sans difficulté, car leur présence altère les sédiments en cassant la séquence stratigraphique dans des zones concrètes, ce qui produit un mélange d'éléments des activités quotidiennes et d'autres éléments de caractère funéraire, donnant comme résultat une composition étrange. Urtiaga, Kobeaga, Abauntz, Padre Areso, Lumentxa, etc. en sont des cas connus. Dans ces fosses le cadavre est en décubitus dorsal, couché sur un côté ou assis en position verticale (Abauntz). Leur profondeur et leur extension varient suivant chaque cas pouvant atteindre un mètre sous le niveau original (Urtiaga).

Il ne faut pas éliminer l'existence de fosses dans des cavités qui auraient pu servir de manière ponctuelle à des fins exclusivement funéraires.

1b.- Trous dans des endroits à plein air

Ils se conservent dans des endroits à plein air à proximité des villages ou dans les villages mêmes (Los Cascajos). Ils présentent des formes variables (cuvette, fond de sac, etc.), certains d'entre eux ont des couvercles de grès et leurs dimensions oscillent autour d'un mètre de diamètre et une profondeur similaire. Ces structures si simples du point de vue de la forme présentent pourtant des restes matériels (ossements humains, ossements d'animaux, céramiques presque complètes, etc.) qui démontrent un usage varié. Au cours des dernières décennies diverses interprétations ont été réalisées sur l'utilité de ce type de structures (dépôt de poubelles, endroits de stockage, silos, fosses funéraires, etc.), ainsi que sur leur chronologie (depuis le Néolithique jusqu'à l'époque romaine). Jusqu'à présent ces types de structures ont été localisées seulement dans la province de Alava et en Navarre, ce sont les sites à fossés de ce dernier territoire qui nous intéressent ici pour leur fonction funéraire (Los Cascajos, La Facería, Paternanbidea, Aparrea). Il faut pourtant noter que les informations que nous possédons actuellement sont provisoires car elles sont en train d'être étudiées, malgré ce fait les données publiées jusqu'à ce jour nous permettent de déduire la complexité de ce phénomène, le premier de ces sites est le plus complet.

A l'intérieur de ces trous peuvent apparaître des enterrements simples ou doubles et dans certains on trouve des réutilisations ; ainsi un défunt peut apparaître à côté d'un autre ou l'un peut être déposé sur l'autre. La position du cadavre est normalement fœtale, il est couché sur un côté et, dans le cas de Los Cascajos, orienté vers l'ouest.

Ce type d'enterrement peut apparaître isolé ou regroupé, formant des sites à fossés. Dans les cas où les trous apparaissent à l'intérieur des villages ils se situent dans la zone centrale, comme semble être le cas de Los Cascajos. La présence d'objets est assez fréquente dans ces tombes, 65,6% en continnent, ce sont principalement des objets en céramique (imprimée, incise, etc.), mais les éléments décoratifs sont rares.

2a.- Dépots en surface, sans aucune structure, à l'intérieur de grottes sépulcrales et d'abris

Ils se conservent dans des grottes et des abris de caractère sépulcral et mixte (habitation/funéraire) simultané ou non.

Ils se caractérisent car ils contiennent une grande quantité d'ossements humains, fréquemment mélangés et généralement sans connections anatomiques. Les défunts étaient placés en surface, mais bien qu'il n'y ait pas de preuves très nettes qui soient conservées, les cadavres étaient probablement isolés de leur environnement en les couvrant avec de la terre, des pierres (comme un genre de tumulus), des structures légères, etc.

Dans le cas de grottes avec une utilisation mixte simultanée il est évident que cette pratique était commune. De plus, comme la recherche d'un endroit caché est une caractéristique commune à tous les endroits d'enterrements, il paraît évident que ces enceintes sépulcrales étaient sellées dans le but d'éviter la spoliation par des bêtes.

Dans les caves à caractère uniquement sépulcral les restent gisent sur des surfaces semi-couvertes.

Dans les caves et abris mixtes d'utilisation non simultanée les restes sont couverts par des niveaux d'utilisations différentes, soit comme refuges temporaires (Peña Larga, Abauntz, etc.) soit comme des étables (Los Husos I).

Le nombre de défunts qu'ils contiennent est très variable. Ils existent des cas comme San Juan Ante Portam Latinam qui contiennent les restes de 289 individus, Pico Ramos 104, Las Yurdinas 87 ou Gobaederra 81, ce qui donne l'impression que ce sont des endroits d'enterrement stables ou en usage permanent. D'un autre côté il y a beaucoup d'endroits où le nombre d'individus est très réduit ; par exemple Los Husos I et Marizulo ont 4 individus. Fuente Hoz 9, Arantzazu 2, Urtiaga 6, ou Padre Areso 2 de chronologies différentes.

Etant donné le caractère désordonné des ossements il est très difficile de chercher une orientation ou une constante en relation avec la manière de placer les défunts. Dans certains cas on a pu vérifier qu'au moins les derniers enterrés étaient placés vers le soleil levant (Peña Larga).

2b.1- Cistes à l'intérieur de refuges naturels : Marizulo et Abauntz

On appelle cistes de petits espaces funéraires délimités par des dalles (Marizulo), des blocs de pierre ou des murets de brique (Abauntz) qui peuvent se trouver à l'intérieur de grottes et d'abris rocheux. Les cistes peuvent être formés soit par des blocs de pierre (Marizulo), soit par des constructions de briques (Abauntz). Dans les deux cas il pourrait s'agir d'endroits à fonction mixte, et peut-être simultanée, Marizulo a une chronologie Néolithique et Abauntz Chalcolithique, leurs caractéristiques formelles peuvent obéir à un essai d'isoler le défunt de son entourage.

Dans le cas de Abauntz le ciste était couvert par une dalle en grès, on signale aussi l'existence de pierres qui auraient pu être enfoncées verticalement dans le sol à la manière d'une stèle.

2b.2- Dolmens et cistes à l'air libre

Les types de dolmens les plus caractéristiques du Pays Basque sont : les dolmens simples (selon d'autres appelés coffres ou cistes dû aux dimensions réduites de la majorité d'entre eux), les sépulcres de couloir, les sépulcres à dalle perforée, les galeries couvertes (rares et peu caractéristiques) et les cistes de tradition dolménique.

Les dolmens simples représentent autour de 90% du total des nécropoles (nombre qui atteint à peu près 600 exemplaires). Ils sont situés dans toutes les zones de montagne du Pays Basque, leur concentration varie beaucoup d'un territoire à l'autre. On n'en connaît pas ou il n'y en a pas de conservés dans la moitié sud de la Navarre y ils sont peu représentés dans le sud de la province d'Alava et dans les zones calcaires de Bizkaia et Gipuzkoa- sierra de Izarraitz et secteur occidental de la province-). Comme on le dit traditionnellement la majorité se trouve sur des collines, sur des replats situés sur les versants, sur des lignes de partage des eaux, en relation avec des chemins pastoraux, dans des zones de grande visibilité, etc. et leur emplacement a tendance à coïncider avec les zones les plus élevées de chaque endroit. Récemment on en a trouvé dans des zones jusqu'ici considérées atypiques comme par exemple des versants de montagne ou des vallées. En général, il n'y a pas de concentrations de dolmens, bien qu'on les trouve parfois par deux (Gorostiaran, Trikuaizti, etc.).

Pour ces monuments il s'agit de sépulcres de dimensions réduites, très fréquemment avec des chambres dont la longueur intérieure ne dépasse pas les deux mètres et des dalles de dimensions réduites. La forme de l'enceinte sépulcrale a tendance à être rectangulaire, trapézoïdale ou polygonale. Pourtant on trouve aussi des exemplaires avec des dalles de plusieurs tonnes (Aranzadi, etc.) et plus longues (Beotegiko Murkoa et Mandubi Zelaia avec certaines dalles de plus de 3 mètres.).

La chambre est d'habitude entourée par une structure tumulaire construite avec des blocs et des dalles de pierres posées de manière plus ou moins organisée Elle se réduit la plupart du temps en disposant les blocs les plus grands à la base, parfois imbriqués entre eux et orientés vers le centre (Trikuaizti I, Zorroztarri, Praalata, etc.). Dans certaines occasions, des blocs de pierres sont disposés dans la partie périphérique, enfoncés dans la terre à la manière des péristyles ou en forme circulaire. Ensuite il y a des pierres plus petites, posées ou jetées jusqu'à donner au tumulus une forme de demi-sphère. Le diamètre atteint peu souvent les 20 mètres, généralement il se situe aux alentours de 12 à 16 mètres. La hauteur réelle est normalement inférieure à un mètre.

Les différences et variations décrites ici ne sont pas le résultat d'une évolution, mais probablement la conséquence des caractéristiques des matières premières qui étaient les plus proches et des besoins du groupe humain qui les a construites. La technique de construction est très simple et répétitive.

La chronologie initiale de ces monuments, en base a la date apportée par les charbons infra tumulaires, se situe autour

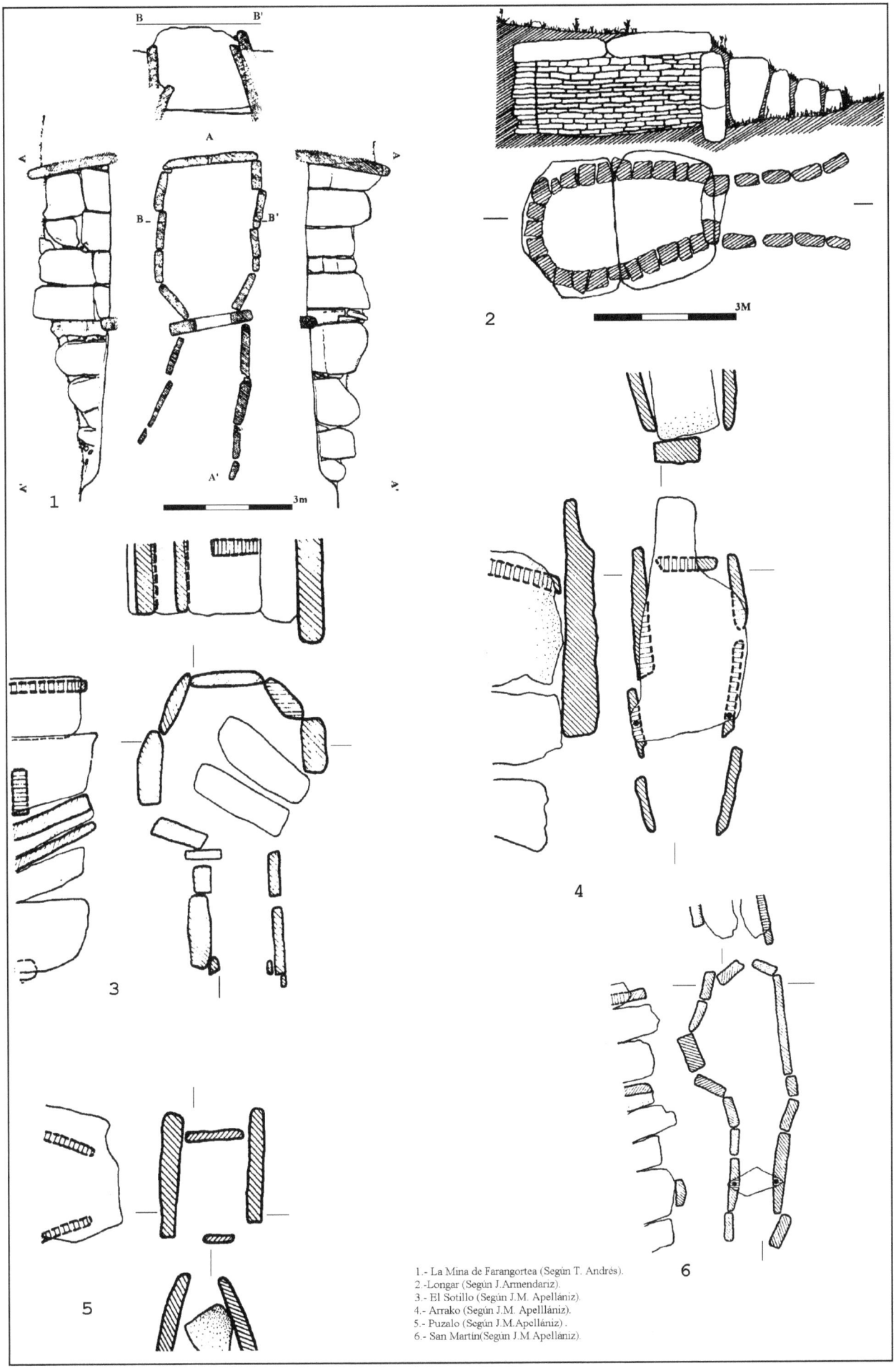

Figure 2.

de 5200 BP, elle coïncide ainsi avec les dates des dolmens de couloir. On constate aussi la construction de nouveaux monuments pendant la seconde moitié du III millénaire. av. J.C. (pas calibré) et les réutilisations au moins jusqu'à la seconde moitié du II millénaire.

En étroite relation avec les dolmens, autant pour l'espace géographique qu'ils occupent que pour la similitude de leurs formes, nous trouvons d'autres structures funéraires que nous dénommons cistes de tradition dolméniques. Leurs dimensions sont encore plus réduites que celles des dolmens simples, car elle atteignent à peine un mètre de long et un demi mètre de large (Atxurbi, Aitxu, etc.), ils partagent certaines de leurs caractéristiques (entourés d'un petit tumulus, parfois très réduit, qui est construit de manière très similaire à celle des dolmens), mais présentent quelques différences, par exemple : on les a élevés en en prenant un plus grand soin, ils sont initialement construits par un individu de prestige, il n'y a pas d'objets dans la chambre ou quand il y en a- dans la chambre ou sous le tumulus- ils sont très caractéristiques et les exemplaires datés les situent à l'Age du Bronze (pour l'instant dans la 1ère moitié du II millénaire a. de C.).Quelques uns se situent à côté d'un dolmen classique (Atxurbi, Aitxu), alors que d'autres (Mulisko, Gaiña) sont à côté de " baratzak " (cromlech) ou de cercles de pierres de caractère funéraire de l'Age de Fer.

Les sépulcres de couloir constituent l'autre ensemble significatif avec une vingtaine de cas, la majorité situés sur les rives de l'Ebre (San Martin, Chabola de la Hechicera, El Sotillo, Los Llanos, Layaza et Peciña) au sud de Sierra Cantabria, et dans d'autres zones de la province de Alava (La Mina de Salcedo, Los Andrinales, Aizkomendi et Sorginetxe (?), Gurpide (?), et San Sebastian. A part ces groupements de zones de vallées nous avons des exemplaires isolés dans des zones de montagne comme Igartza W, et en plus certains qui sont un peu douteux comme Etxarriko Portugañe et Legaire S.

La chambre de ces types de dolmens est d'habitude rectangulaire ou polygonale et les couloirs sont généralement courts (il semble que Aizkomendi avait 7 mètres de long et Igartza W seulement 1,5 mètres.). Leurs tumulus de pierre ont en général des dimension discrètes (les 64 mètres de Aizkomendi sont exceptionnels). Les matériaux de construction proviennent de l'entourage du dolmen. L'exception est que Aizkomendi a des dalles calcaires qui ont été amenées d'une distance supérieure à un kilomètre, et d'autres en grès transportées depuis une distance de presque 6 kilomètres.

Leur chronologie initiale les situe vers 5300 BP et il y a des dates d'ossements humains de 5100 BP. Il faut signaler que l'architecture et les objets de la première phase mégalithique (de préférence idoles-spatules et objets géométriques) sont en connexion avec beaucoup des sépulcres connus dans La Rioja et la Meseta Norte, bien qu'il existe des différences (dimensions, orientation, etc.) comme conséquence, probablement, de l'adaptation aux caractéristiques géologiques de l'endroit et à celles de la société qui les érige et de la tradition culturelle. Leur utilisation se prolonge jusqu'à l'Age du Bronze.

Les sépulcres à dalle perforée, pour certains proches des sépulcres de galeries, se caractérisent par la présence d'une dalle perforée située à la porte de la chambre. Les trois exemplaires connus se situent dans la moitié sud de la Navarre (La Mina de Farangortea, Portillo de Eneriz et Longar). La chambre est rectangulaire dans les deux premiers et elle est construite avec des dalles posées verticalement, alors que celle de Longar est elliptique et ceci au moyen d'un mur de blocs de pierres. Les indices de travail effectué en ciselant la dalle perforée sont importants.

Il n'existe pas une opinion unanime entre les chercheurs sur leur origine, ils la cherchent dans le sud et sud-est de l'Espagne, en Catalogne, ou dans le sud-est de la France et leur possible relation avec la culture du S.O.M n'est pas claire elle non plus.

Leur chronologie est plus récente que celle des dolmens simples et des dolmens de couloir, elle se situe en 4700 BP dans le cas de Longar. Leurs dernières réutilisations s'attribuent à l'Age du Bronze.

4. LE MOBILIER FUNÉRAIRE

La première difficulté est celle de la définition de ce que l'on entend par mobilier funéraire, car les mêmes objets, dépendant du contexte (variable suivant la modalité d'enterrement) et de leur interprétation peuvent être inclus ou non. Pour nous, on ne peut nier qu'un type d'objets funéraires existe, on peut considérer comme tels les bols de Lumentxa, les idoles spatules de San Martin et Gorutxebide, les burins et les poignards de Gobaederra, le chien et le mouton de Marizulo, le crane de chien de San Juan Ante Portan Latinam et les crayons d'ocre de Praalata, Zorrostarri et Ithe sont probablement en relation avec un type de rituel.

On constate la présence d'objets de manière assez systématique dans les sépulcres en fosses (Los Cascajos, etc.), puisque 65,6% en contiennent. Ces objets sont composés principalement par des récipients en céramique, la présence d'objets de décoration personnelle est assez rare. Dans les quelques cas contrôlés dans d'autres contextes Néolithiques (grottes de Lumentxa et Marizulo), dans des dates comprises entre le V° et IV° millénaire A. de C. (non calibré), il semble que la présence d'objets soit plus systématique que dans les époques postérieures.

Dans les enterrements dans des grottes ou des abris d'habitation il existe des situations différentes :

– dans un cas, les enterrements en fosses fouillés présentent en général un mélange de possibles objets funéraires et de restes archéologiques des nivaux archéologiques qui sont coupés ou altérés durant la réalisation de la fosse.

– dans l'autre cas, les dépots en surface. Dans ce cas on ne peut pas non plus savoir quel objets correspondent à chaque défunt, s'il en existe, car en général ceux qui les ont déposés les ont mélangés eux-même ou alors ils se sont mélangés pour des causes naturelles (bêtes sauvages, animaux charognards, etc.).

Dans le cas des cavités d'utilisation exclusivement funéraire (Yurdinas, Iruaxpe I, Urtao, etc.) la problématique est similaire á celle décrite dans le dernier paragraphe.

Les fouilles archéologiques ont permis d'observer que les matériaux archéologiques se récupèrent dams des contextes différents. Les uns sont récupérés à la surface du tumulus (parfois dans l'intérieur de la structure tumulaire) et ils sont composés par des éclats de pierres, des fragments laminaires et des outils de substrat (grattoirs, perçoirs, etc.) fabriqués pour des activités de type domestique. Dans certains cas (Trikuaizti I, Zorroztarri) on arrive à constater la manufacture d'instruments sur le propre tumulus. Ces objets ne peuvent pas se considéré proprement dit comme des objets d'enterrement et seuls quelques uns de ceux qui procèdent de l'intérieur de la chambre se considéreront comme tels, d'un autre côté on observe un changement radical dans la composition typologique des éléments par la présence d'objets de décoration personnelle et d'armatures lithiques qui ont pu arriver involontairement à l'enceinte sépulcrale. Dans ce cas, le contexte est clair mais l'intentionnalité de leur présence ne l'est pas tant. Pourtant il est difficile d'expliquer la présence d'autres objets sans supposer qu'il s'agisse d'offrandes. Ceci pourrait être le cas des récipients céramiques relativement complets comme les vases lisses de Ausokoi, Mandubi Zelaia ; les campaniformes de Tres Montes, Pagobakoitza, El Sotillo, Los Llanos, Trikuaizti I ou le vase polydope avec des décorations cordées de Urdanarre. La présence de certains objets peu habituels sous le tumulus pourraient aussi être un indice de la possibilité des offrandes : la hache polie de Trikuaizti I, le poignard en silex de Aitxu, etc.

Il faut signaler qu'il ne semble pas qu'il y ait des objets d'enterrement typiques en relation avec le sexe, l'âge, le prestige social, etc., on peut même arriver à se demander si les objets récupérés sont réellement des objets d'enterrement ou s'ils sont arrivés de forme involontaire dans le corps du défunt. D'un autre côté, si cela avait existé, il devrait y avoir des variations dans la composition au cours du temps comme résultat des transformations socio-économiques et des changements de mentalité de la population. Une preuve de ceci c'est que dans les enterrements néolithiques dans des fosses (Los Cascajos, etc.) et dans des grottes (Marizulo, Lumentxa) la présence d'objets d'enterrement est plus fréquente que dans les tombes postérieures.

Dans certaines occasions, la concentration d'un type d'éléments déterminé (objets métalliques de Gobaederra, le lingot de cuivre de Urtiaga, les idoles-spatules de S. Martin ou Kurutzebide, etc.) pourraient être le témoignage d'offrandes faites à des individus concrets de la population.

En plus de la présence d'objets manufacturés il y a des preuves d'offrandes d'animaux, qui dans la mesure où ils montrent des indices d'intentionnalité peuvent être acceptés sans aucun doute. Ce serait le cas de l'agneau et du chien de Marizulo ou du crâne de chien de San Juan Ante Portam Latinam. D'autres exemples d'ossements d'ongulés dans des dolmens (Ausokoi, Kurutzebide, Luperta, Oidui, etc.) ou de chiens (Seakoain, Debata del Realengo) ne sont pas assez évidents car il s'agit de fouilles anciennes et leur situation à l'intérieur de la chambre n'a pas été contrôlée.

Il semble que les crayons d'ocre cités dans certains dolmens (Praalata, Zorroztarri, Ithé) puissent être en relation avec le rituel, la coloration rougeâtre de certains ossements humains pourrait en être un indice.

La pratique d'autres rituels comme celui d'inutiliser des objets métalliques, que dans certaines occasions J.M. Barandiaran citera à cause de la présence de burins métalliques courbés dans les dolmens de La Cañada-Urbasa- et Gorostiaran E-Aizkorri-, ne semble pas avoir été habituelle non plus et dans les cas que l'on connaît semble être simplement accidentelle. Pourtant on semble constater cette pratique de manière assez systématique en Aquitaine et dans le monde celtibérique durant l'Age du Fer.

Il faut indiquer qu'il semble que, malgré les différentes modalités d'enterrement décrites il n'existe pas d'objets d'enterrement différenciés entre eux. C'est seulement les objets en or, les céramiques campaniformes internationales et les idoles spatules qui semblent s'inscrire dans des contextes funéraires dolméniques. Il faut pourtant signaler la disproportion existante entre le numéro de dolmens fouillés et celui des grottes sépulcrales, et aussi le nombre limité de ces dernières entre la fin du IV millénaire et la première moitié de III pourrait expliquer ce déséquilibre.

Une autre série de possibles rituels comme les offrandes de lumière et de feu dans des contextes dolméniques doivent être considérés avec des réserves dans la majorité des cas car ils n'ont pas été datés. En fait, certaines citations de J.M. Barandiaran, relatives à ces rituels dans des dolmens de Ataun-Borunda- par exemple- peuvent se questionner vu que les fouilles de certains d'entre eux (Igartza W) et leur postérieure datation démontrent qu'il s'agit d'incendies ou de feux antérieurs à leur construction.

Finalement, il faut indiquer que depuis les plus anciennes fouilles réalisées dans la région Basque on signale un rite de crémation associé à des ensembles d'ossements humains. Pourtant, dans les fouilles réalisées dans certaines cavités (Peña Larga, Las Yurdinas et même Abauntz) durant les dernières décades on constate que cette habitude de brûler les restes humains semble obéir plus à une tâche d'hygiène postérieure à la déposition qu'à une action liée à l'acte du rituel funéraire en soi. Dans certains de ces cas on trouve un niveau d'occupation au-dessus de celui des enterrements brûlés ; à Peña Larga le niveau d'enterrement (chalcolithique Ancien) a été brûlé et sellé avec des pierres par ceux qui ont employé l'endroit comme un refuge quelques années après (chalcolithique Avancé-final) qu'il ait servi de dépôt funéraire.

5. ECONOMIE ET MODES DE VIE

A la lumière des dernières recherches il commence à exister des preuves bien fondées que le développement de l'économie productive est plus vieille que ce qu'on avait supposé et que mêmes les différences entre la zone holohumide supposée très retardataire et les autres zones de la vallée de l'Ebre ne sont probablement pas si importantes.

La domestication dans la Vallée Haute de l'Ebre semble être quelque chose qui est importé depuis la Méditerranée orientale atteignant peu à peu des zones de plus en plus orientales et intérieures. Ainsi, dans la zone moyenne de la Vallée de l'Ebre on détecte la présence d'une cabane domestique (bovidés, ovins-caprins et porcs) dès le début du V° millénaire (Chaves, Cueva del Moro de Olvena, etc.) Sur le versant méditerranéen du Pays Basque dès la fin du V° millénaire comme le montrent les gisements de Los Husos I (6240±60 BP) et Peña Larga (6150±230 BP). Dans la zone de la côte à des dates antérieures à la moiié du IV° millénaire, ce qu'on peut vérifier dans le niveau V du gisement de Kobaederra (Kortezubi) (le niveau IV a été daté en 5630±100 BP) ou dans le ICI de Arenaza. Pendant cette même époque on trouve de la faune domestique dans la zone pre –pyrénéenne dans la grotte de Abauntz.

Dans les études réalisées pendant les dernières années on insiste sur les types et la provenance des silex qui apparaissent dans les gisements archéologiques. De cette manière on peut déduire une importante relation nord-sud entre le littoral et la Haute Vallée de l'Ebre. Cette hypothèse initiale démontrée par la présence importante de silex de Urbasa, de Treviño ou de l'Ebre dans des gisements de la côte de guipuzcoa (Herriko Barra, megalitos, etc.). Il est évident que le besoin de s'approvisionner en silex (Tarriño, A.) dans les affleurements les plus grands du territoire (Treviño, Urbasa et flysch) aurait eu comme conséquence la rapide expansion de connaissances nouvelles et de développements qui auraient pu exister en articulant le territoire de cette manière.

Avec l'arrivée de chalcolithique l'activité de l'élevage dans la zone ne diminue pas, au contraire elle semble se renforcer encore plus. Dans la Rioja Alavesa, une série d'abris sous roche s'ouvrent qui seront prospectés dans les dernières années (Peña Larga, Los HusosI, Los Husos II et San Cristobal). On a pu y identifier des niveaux de stabulation qui contienent des restes de bercail ou d'enclos où on pouvait enfermer le bétail. Le cas le plus frappant correspond sans doute à Los Husos I où on a trouvé trois trous de piliers qui conservent un empilement de boue durcie par une hyper collation de carbonates et de pierres autour d'eux. Ils ont dû faire partie d'une clôture qui fermait l'ample ouverture de l'abri. A l'intérieur on a trouvé d'importantes extensions de carbonates et de grès dilué, des restes de zones qui ont dû être inondées, de petits niveaux noir très plastiques, des ossements et des restes de céramiques non brûlés. L'analyse chimique de ces sédiments détermine une grande quantité de phosphore, très peu de fer et de hautes proportions d'autres métaux comme le zinc. Le même type de sédiment a été trouvé dans l'abri de San Cristobal avec une analytique très similaire et à Peña Larga. Dans l'abri de Los Husos II on a détecté un niveau de stabulation de la même époque que les précédents bien que dans ce cas se produisent des accumulations de grandes quantités de cendres. Il se peut qu'à cet endroit il se produise un assainissement périodique de l'étable en le brûlant, ce qui n'arrive pas dans les autres abris proches. La pratique de brûler les étables a été très courante jusqu'à l'époque récente et on l'a détectée, dans des étapes préhistoriques, en bordure de méditerranée depuis la Grèce jusqu'à la Péninsule Ibérique. De cette manière on peut observer comment à partir du chalcolithique les abris qui jalonnent la Sierra Cantabrica acquièrent la fonction de bercail au détriment de celle l'habitation ou de l'enterrement qu'ils avaient eu auparavant.

En ce qui concerne l'agriculture il est très compliqué de trouver des restes de pollens fossiles de l'étape de l'ancien Néolithique, dans les abris et les grottes où l'on a détecté cette période. Leur situation dans des zones élevées en relation avec la vallée rend difficile que des pollens domestiques qui sont plus lourds que les pollens sylvestres puissent arriver jusque là. Dans certains gisements de chronologie ancienne, situés dans des zones de vallées, on a cité la présence de céréales brûlées dans l'intérieur des fosses funéraires (Los Cascajos). Les résultats de ces recherches seront d'une grande importance à l'heure de déterminer les connaissances sur le néolithique dans toute la zone.

Il est commun de considérer que les dolmens de vallée, élevés dans des zones avec une tradition de culture de céréales qui remonte à une époque ancienne, avaient été construits et utilisés par des populations dont l'économie était principalement basée sur l'agriculture.

Pourtant cette vision doit être nuancée car certains sépulcres de couloir ou de dalle perforée ne se trouvent pas dans le contexte le plus adéquat pour cette activité agricole. C'est le cas de Layaza, Txarrakadi, Portillo de Eneritz, La Mina de Farangortea, Longar, etc. Ceux-ci se trouvent en réalité sur les limites marginales des terres les plus riches. Dans un certain sens, ceci viendrait à ratifier le rôle de signes pour délimiter le territoire qu'on avait pour habitude d'assigner à ces dolmens, fréquemment attribués à des populations de bergers transhumants.

Le mégalithisme est un phénomène de longue durée, et évidemment à l'intérieur de celui-ci auraient existés des changements ou des modifications dans ses rituels et dans la signification non fonctionnelle que pourraient avoir les dolmens comme résultat des transformations qu'allait connaître la propre société constructrice ou utilisatrice de ces dolmens.

C'est pour ceci qu'il faudrait considérer le caractère saisonnier de l'utilisation de beaucoup de dolmens (de préférence les simples) et des grottes sépulcrales de certaines montagnes. Les usagers du dolmen situé dans les pâturages d'été en utiliseraient d'autres situés sur leur route de transhumance à des altitudes moins élevées ou même ont-ils pu être inhumés dans des fosses creusées dans des endroits situés dans des zones de vallées. Malheureusement, pour le moment, nous n'avons pas de preuves de ce dernier fait, mais se serait l'unique possibilité de comprendre de manière logique et cohérente le peuplement et le monde funéraire de cette époque.

Une des caractéristiques du rituel funéraire serait sa complexité et sa diversité. Face à une homogénéité et une unité supposées de ce phénomène dans le territoire que l'on étudie nous trouvons des formes variées d'enterrement (grottes, fosses, mégalithes, etc.).

Adresse des auteurs

J. FERNANDEZ ERASO
J.A. MUJIKA ALUSTIZA
Faculté de Philologie, Géographie et Histoire
Universidad del País Vasco/euskal Herriko Unibertsitatea
C/ Tomás y Valiente s/n.
01006 Vitoria-Gasteiz ESPAGNE

Bibliographie

ALDAY. A., 1998. *El depòsito prehistórico de Kanpanoste Goikoa (Vírgala, Alava). Memoria de las actuaciones arqueológicas. 1992 y 1993)* Memorias de yacimientos alavese n° 5. Vitoria.

ANDRES, M.T., 1977. Las estructuras funerarias del Neolítico y Eneolítico en la Cuenca Media del Ebro. Consideraciones críticas. *Príncipe de Viana* 146-147, 65-127. Pamplona.

ANDRES, M.T., 1979. Ritos funerarios de la Cuenca Media del Ebro: Neolítico y Eneolítico. *Berceo* 97,3-25. Logroño.

ANDRES, M.T., 1986. El megalitismo en el Pirineo Occidental. *Actas de la Mesa Redonda sobre Megalitismo Peninsular* (1984), 133 -144. Madrid.

ANDRES, M.T., 1990. El fenómeno dolménico en el País Vasco. *Munibe* 42, 141-152. Donostia.

ANDRES, M.T., 1998. *Colectivismo funerario neo-eneolítico. Aproximación metodológica sobre datos de la cuenca alta y media del Ebro.* 257 págs. Instituto Fernando El Católico. Zaragoza.

ANDRES, M.T., GARCIA, Mª.L., & SESMA, J., 1997. El sepulcro calcolítico de Tres Montes (Las Bardenas Reales, Navarra). *II Congreso de Arqueología Peninsular*, 301-308.

APELLANIZ, J.M., 1973. Corpus de materiales de las culturas prehistóricas con cerámica de la población de cavernas del País Vasco. *Munibe*, 366 pp. Donostia.

APELLANIZ, J.M., 1974. El Grupo de los Husos durante la Prehistoria con cerámica. *Estudios de Arqueología Alavesa* 7, 1-409. Vitoria.

APELLANIZ, J.M., 1975. El Grupo de Santimamiñe durante la Prehistoria con cerámica. *Munibe* 27, 1-136. Donostia.

APELLANIZ, J.M., FERNANDEZ MEDRANO, D., 1978. El sepulcro de galería segmentada de la Chabola de la Hechicera (Elvillar, Alava). Excavación y restauración. *Estudios de Arqueología Alavesa* 9, 141-224. Vitoria.

ARANZADI, T., ANSOLEAGA, F., 1915. *Exploración de cinco dólmenes del Aralar.* Diputación de Navarra, Pamplona.

ARANZADI, T., ANSOLEAGA, F., 1918. *Exploración de catorce dólmenes del Aralar.* Diputación de Navarra, Pamplona.

ARANZADI, T., BARANDIARAN, J.M., EGUREN, E., 1919. Exploración de seis dólmenes de la sierra de Aizkorri. *Obras Completas* VII, 251-341.

ARANZADI, T., BARANDIARAN, J.M., EGUREN, E., 1921. Exploración de ocho dólmenes de Altzania. *Obras Completas* VIII, 11-83.

ARANZADI, T., BARANDIARAN, J.M., EGUREN, E., 1921. Los nuevos dólmenes de la Sierra de Encia. *Obras Completas* VIII. 83-101.

ARANZADI, T., BARANDIARAN, J.M., EGUREN, E., 1921. Exploración de diez y seis dólmenes de la sierra de Elosua-Plazentzia. *Obras Completas* VIII. 101-135.

ARANZADI, T., BARANDIARAN, J.M., EGUREN, E., 1921. Exploración de seis dólmenes de la sierra de Urbasa (Navarra). *Obras Completas* VIII. 167-239.

ARMENDARIZ MARTIJA, J., IRIGARAY SOTO, S., 1993. Resumen de las excavaciones arqueológicas en el hipogeo de Longar (Viana, Navarra). 1991-1993. *Arqueología Navarra* 11, 270-275. Pamplona.

ARMENDARIZ MARTIJA, J., IRIGARAY SOTO, S., 1994. *La arquitectura de la muerte. El hipogeo de Longar (Viana, Navarra), un sepulcro colectivo del 2500 a.C.* 36 pp. Centro de Estudios Tierra-Estella, Lizarraldeko Ikastetxea.

BARANDIARAN, J.M., 1966-68. Exploración de Aizkomendi (Dolmen de Eguilaz, Alava). *Noticiario Arqueológico Hispánico* X-XI y XII, 97-109.

BARANDIARAN, J.M., FERNANDEZ MEDRANO, D; APELLANIZ, J.Mª. 1964, Excavación del dolmen deSan Martín (Laguardia). *Obras Completas* XVI, 29-73.

EBRARD, D., 1993. Architectures, stratigraphies et foctionnements des dolmens I et II d'Ithé (Assurucq, Pyrénées-Atlantiques). *Société d'Anthropologie du Sud-Ouest* XXVIII (Colloque Megalithes du Sud-Ouest, 1992), 151-179.

FERNANDEZ ERASO, J., 1997. *Excavaciones en Peña Larga*-MEMORIAS de yacimientos alaveses n°.4 Vitoria.

FERNANDEZ ERASO, J., 1999. Excavaciones en el Abrigo de Los Husos I (Elvillar). *Arkeoikuska*'99. Pp.44-49.Vitoria

FERNANDEZ ERASO, J., 1999. Prospecciones en la Sierra de Cantabria. *Arkeoikuska*'99. Pp.53 Vitoria.

FERNANDEZ ERASO, J., 1999. Excavaciones. Cueva de Las Yurdinas II. *Arkeoikuska*'99. Pp.54-57. Vitoria

FERNANDEZ ERASO, J., 2000. Excavaciones. Abrigo de Los Husos I (Elvillar). *Arkeoikuska*'00. Pp.39-45. Vitoria.

FERNANDEZ ERASO, J., 2000. Excavaciones. Abrigo de San Cristóbal (Laguardia) *Arkeoikuska*'00. Pp.47-50. Vitoria.

FERNANDEZ ERASO, J., 2000. Excavaciones. Las Yurdinas II. (Peñacerrada). *Arkeoikuska*'00. Pp.52-56. Vitoria.

GARCIA GAZOLAZ, J., SESMA SESMA, J., 1999. Talleres de sílex versus lugares de habitación. Los Cascajos (Los Arcos, Navarra), un ejemplo de neolitización en el Alto Valle del Ebro. II Congrès del Neolithic a la Península Ibèrica, *Saguntum-PLAV* Extra 2, 343-350.

LOPEZ DE CALLE, C., 1992. Tratamientos sepulcrales y presepulcrales de restos humanos en los Yacimientos megalíticos de Cameros. *Estrato* 4, 36-41.

LOPEZ DE CALLE, C., 1994. Caracteres arquitectónicos y restos materiales del sepulcro megalítico de Collado del Mallo (Trevijano). *Estrato* 6, 9-15. Logroño.

LOPEZ DE CALLA, C., ILARRAZA, J.A., 1997. Condenaciones y remodelaciones. Una respuesta a las estratigrafíasde los sepulcros megalíticos de Cameros. *II Congreso de Arqueología Peninsular*, 309-320.

MUJIKA ALUSTIZA, J.A., 1993. Aportaciones durante el último decenio al conocimiento del fenómeno dolménico de Gipuzkoa. *Société d'Anthropologie du Sud-Ouest* XXVIII (Colloque Megalithes du Sud-Ouest, 1992), 205-225.

MUJIKA ALUSTIZA, J.A., 1994. Los dólmenes simples del País Vasco. Aspectos constructivos y cronológicos. *Ilunzar* 2, 9-20, Asociación Cultural de Arqueología Agiri, Gernika.

MUJIKA ALUSTIZA, J.A., 1998. Ídolos-espátulas del País Vasco: fabricación, cronología y paralelos. *Veleia* 15, 121-145.

MUJIKA ALUSTIZA, J.A., ARMENDARIZ, A., 1991. Excavaciones en la estación megalítica de Murumendi (Beasain, Guipúzcoa). *Munibe* 43, 105-165.

PEREZ ARRONDO, C.L., LOPEZ DE CALLE, C., 1988. Excavaciones en la zona megalítica de Viguera (La Rioja). Collado Palomero I. Campañas de 1986 y 1986. *Cuad. Invest. Hist., Brocar* 14, 31-52.

UTRILLA, P., MAZO, C., 1993-94. Informe preliminar sobre la actuación de urgencia de 1991 en la cueva de Abauntz. *Trabajos de Arqueología Navarra* 11, 10-29.

VEGAS ARAMBURU, J.I., 1981. Túmulo-dolmen de Kurtzebide en Letona. Memoria de excavación. *Estudios de Arqueología Alavesa* 10, 19-67. Vitoria.

VEGAS ARAMBURU, J.I., 1999. *El enterramiento neolítico de San Juan Ante Portam Latinam.* 129 pp. Arabako Foru Diputazioa.

VEGAS ARAMBURU, J.I., MARTINEZ-TORRES, L.M., ORUE-ETXEBERRIA, X., GARCIA GAMILLA, F., 1992. Procedencia de las rocas empleadas en la construcción del dolmen de Aizkomendi (Eguilaz, Alava). *The Late Quaternary in the Western Pyrenean Region.* 427-433. UPV/EHU, Vitoria.

VIVANCO, J.J., 1981. Orientación y tipología de las cámaras de los dólmenes de montaña y valle. *Estudios de Arqueología Alavesa* 10, 67-145. Vitoria.

YARRITU, M.J., GORROTXATEGI, X., 199, "La Cabaña 4" trikuharrian burututako azterketa arkeologikoari buruzko txostena, Karrantza, 1979-82. Egitura eta material arkeologikoak. *Isturitz* 10, 206-233.

TYPE	DATE	GISEMENT
As.aa	4250±110	La Renke
As.aa	4400±100	"
As.aa	4410±100	"
As.aa	4590±100	"
As.aa	4600±100	"
As.aa	5180±100	"
As.aa	5210±100	"
As.aa	6650±130	Pareko Landa
As.aa	5960±95	Herriko Barra
As.aa	6010±90	"
As.aa	3270±90	S. Pelayo
As.ab	3360±100	Marijuan 1
As.ab	3410±40	Los Husos I
As.ab	3610±60	La Peña
As.ab	3630±40	Los Husos I
As.ab	3710±40	"
As.ab	3710±60	La Peña
As.ab	3920±100	Los Husos I
As.ab	4190±40	San Cristóbal
As.ab	4190±100	Kanpanoste G.
As.ab	4350±60	"
As.ab	4350±80	La Peña
As.ab	5400±100	Los Husos II
As.ab	5430±60	Padre Areso
As.ab	5630±60	Los Husos II
As.ab	5810±60	Los Husos I
As.ab	5830±110	Peña Larga
As.ab	6130±60	Los Husos I
As.ab	6150±230	Peña Larga
As.ab	6240±60	Los Husos I
As.ab	6360±60	Kanpanoste G.
As.ab	6370±70	Aizpea
As.ab	6440±40	Mendandia
As.ab	6540±70	"
As.ab	6550±260	Kanpanoste G.
As.ab	6830±70	Aizpea
Asc	3710±100	Solacueva
Asc	4200±130	Anton Koba
Asc	4965±195	Arenaza
Asc	5200±110	Kobaederra

TYPE	DATE	GISEMENT
Asc	5235±75	Marizulo
Asc	5630±100	Kobaederra
Asc	5755±65	Arenaza
Asc	5820±240	Kobaederra
Asc	5860±65	Pico Ramos
Asc	6035±100	Marizulo
Asc	6040±75	Arenaza
Asc	6320±280	Zatoya
Asc	6425±85	Marizulo
Asc	6820±150	"
Asc	6910±450	Abauntz
Asc.	6945±65	Kobeaga II
C.h: as	3170±70	Aparrea
C.h: as	4090	La Facería
C.h: ent	3080±50	Aparrea
C.h:?	3325±30	Cuesta de la Igl.
Cista	3530±110	Aitxu
D	4080±100	Tres Montes
D	4445±95	Kurtzebide
Ds	1495±50	Bernalta 1
Ds	2905±55	"
Ds	3460±50	Aizibita
Ds	3500±140	Ithé 2
Ds	3510±100	"
Ds	3610±120	"
Ds	3920±75	Larrarte
Ds	3960±45	Mandubi Zelaia
Ds	3990±40	Aizibita
Ds	4000±110	Ithé 2
Ds	4030±60	Aizibita
Ds	4155±75	Larrarte
Ds	4310±110	Praalata
Ds	4345±45	Mandubi Zelaia
Ds	4410±50	Aizibita
Ds	4490±50	"
Ds	4865±90	Hirumugarrieta 2
Ds	4950±45	Mandubi Zelaia
Ds	4955±85	Hirumugarrieta 2
Ds	4960±90	Cotobasero 2
Ds	5070±140	Larrarte
Ds	5200±75	Boheriza 2
Ds	5300±140	Trikuaizti 1
Ds	5405±65	La Cabaña 2
Ds	5500±100	Boheriza 2

TYPE	DATE	GISEMENT
Ds	5810±290	Larrarte
D-C	3850±90	Irau IV (Irati)
Eia	3020±35	Padre Areso
Eia	6600±50	Aizpea
Eic	5285±65	Marizulo
Eic	5315±100	"
Ebr	4200±95	San Juan A.P.L.
Ebr	4325±70	"
Ebr	4440±40	"
Ebr	4460±40	"
Ebr	4510±40	"
Ebr	4520±50	"
Ebr	4520±75	"
Ebr	4570±40	"
Ebr	5020±140	"
Ebr	5020±140	"
Nsa	3980±40	Los Husos I
Nsa	4730±110	"
Nsc	3090±100	Guerrandijo
Nsc	3430±100	Urtiaga
Nsc	3445±110	"
Nsc	3475±120	"
Nsc	3660±100	Gobaederra
Nsc	3710±130	Las Pajucas
Nsc	3810±65	Nardoste IV
Nsc	4100±110	Pico Ramos
Nsc	4130±110	Iruaxpe
Nsc	4210±110	Pico Ramos
Nsc	4240±140	Abauntz
Nsc	4290±130	Urtiaga
Nsc	4290±40	Las Yurdinas
Nsc	4335±60	Lacilla II
Nsc	4360±40	Las Yurdinas
Nsc	4370±70	Abauntz
Nsc	4390±80	Las Yurdinas
Nsc	4490±170	Urtao II
Nsc	4585±80	Marizulo
Nsc	4610±120	Urtao II, gal. N.
Nsc	4790±110	Pico Ramos
Nsc	5160±110	Fuente Foz
Nsc	5240±110	"
Nsc	5390±120	Abauntz
P	3220±100	La Hoya
P	3220±90	"

TYPE	DATE	GISEMENT
P	3315±25	Monte Aguilar
P	3315±65	"
P	3330±20	"
P	3380±20	"
P	3410±90	La Hoya
P	3465±35	Puy Aguilar 1
P	3495±35	"
P	3510±100	Monte Aguilar
P	3510±20	"
P	3510±20	"
P	3560±10	"
P	3600±45	"
Sc	4080±170	Los Llanos
Sc	4090±120	"
Sc	4660±200	"
Sc	5190±140	"
Sc	5270±100	Igartza W
Slp	4445±70	Longar
Slp	4480±50	"
Slp	4500±60	"
Slp	4530±60	"
Slp	4540±70	"
Slp	4580±90	"

Abreviatures:
As.ab: Site à plein air
Asc: Site en abris
C.h.as: "Campo de hoyo": site d'habitation
C.h.ent: "Campo de hoyo": site sépulcral
C: Ciste
Ds: Dolmen simple
Nsa: Niveau sépulcral sous abris
Nsc: Niveau sépulcral en grotte
Ebr: Enterrement sous roche
P: Village
Sc: Dolmen à couloir
Slp: Dolmen à dalle à trou
Eia: Enterrement individuel sous abris
Eic: Enterrement individuel en grotte

ON THE LIFE-HISTORIES OF MEGALITHS IN NORTHWEST IBERIA

Marcos MARTINÓN-TORRES

Résumé : La plupart des travaux actuels sur les mégalithes étudient les stades initiaux de leur histoire, leurs origines et premières significations. Néanmoins, il faut compter sur le fait qu'un nombre important de ces monuments est resté dans le paysage pendant des siècles: des sociétés d'époques différentes les ont compris et utilisé dans des voies très diverses. Cet article propose de reconstruire cette diversité d'utilisations et de significations attribuées à ces monuments préhistoriques pendant des époques historiques successives dans le Nord-ouest de la Péninsule Ibérique. Les sources consultées, documentaires et bibliographiques, vont des documents médiévaux jusqu'aux premiers traités de toponymie et d'histoire; on se sert aussi des cadastres modernes, textes juridiques, etc. Comme résultat, on définit trois fonctions principales de ces monuments - territoriale, symbolique et archéologique - et on explore leur évolution dans des contextes divers depuis le Moyen Age jusqu'au XIXe siècle. D'après ces données on insiste sur la nécessité d'étudier non seulement "la naissance", mais aussi toute la "biographie" des mégalithes tout en signalant les implications de ce point de vue pour la pratique archéologique actuelle.

Abstract: Most of the current approaches to megaliths focus on the initial stages of these monuments' histories, their origins and early meanings. However, a significant number of megaliths have remained part of the landscape for many centuries, and different societies from different times have understood and dealt with them in diverse ways. The aim of this paper is to reconstruct these different uses and meanings attributed to the prehistoric monuments during historical times in NW Iberia. The sources used are documentary and bibliographic, ranging from medieval estate record books to the first books of toponymy and history, as well as modern cadastres and a legal case file in which the megaliths are mentioned. As a result, three main roles of the monuments are defined – territorial, symbolic and archaeological -, and their evolution in different social contexts is explored from the Middle Ages to the 19th century AD. On this basis, the necessity of researching not only the 'birth', but the entire 'life-histories' of megaliths is emphasized. The implications of this approach for the current archaeological practice are also outlined.

1. INTRODUCTION

The most common approach to megalithic structures involves their consideration as *containers of archaeological information about megalith builders*. The most frequent questions to be answered usually include when, how and why they were built. Often, conclusions are subsequently drawn on such issues as the social organization, subsistence, ideology or perception of the landscape shared by prehistoric societies. This research approach has yielded valuable results, of which innumerable examples could be cited.

This paper, however, takes a different perspective. Here, megaliths are viewed as *monuments*. This outset accentuates the difference between two distinct issues – on the one hand, the peoples who constructed the megaliths; on the other hand, the megaliths themselves. Monuments have different meanings and uses but are generally intended to last. This applies to megaliths, and in fact this is the main reason why many of them are still present in our landscapes. Accordingly, being distinct entities, the lives of the monument builders are different from the lives of the physical monuments. Megalith builders existed during several centuries in the Later Prehistory. Megaliths were built during several centuries in Later Prehistory, but whilst the society responsible for their construction is no longer, megalithic monuments existed from then through Roman times to the Middle Ages and up until the present day. Thus they have their own life-histories, which only coincided with those of their builders for a relatively short time. For the rest of their existence, the monuments have been engaged with, used and understood in various ways by diverse societies and cultures that happened to co-exist with them. As the societies that had created the monuments disappeared, but the monuments themselves did not, new peoples and new cultures were free to assign them different uses and functions. Hence the monuments underwent various experiences and played assorted roles.

To the best of our knowledge, it was Glyn Daniel (1972) who first explored monument histories. However, only recently this research approach started to be defined and further developed, and its theoretical implications expanded (e.g. Caamaño and Criado 1991-2; Bender 1993; Chippindale 1994; Hingley 1996; Patton 1996; and papers in Bradley and Williams 1998). Particularly notable was Bradley's (1984; 1993; 1996; 2000) concern that the monuments' 'afterlives' be considered, even though he almost exclusively focused on how monuments were used in later periods in order to legitimate a given social order. It is mainly Holtorf (1996; 1997; 1998; 2000-2) who has developed and broadened this approach by studying the 'life-histories of monuments'. Similarly, I have investigated the vicissitudes of 'the megalithic monuments after the megalithic period' (Martinón-Torres and Rodríguez Casal 2000; Martinón-Torres 2001a; 2001b; 2002a). In the present paper, I am explicitly borrowing Holtorf's term, thus partly adhering to his theoretical stance (cf. Holtorf 2000-2, but see my concerns in Martinón-Torres 2002b).

Based on the conviction that the entire histories of megaliths warrant comprehensive attention, this paper focuses on a particular period of the monuments' lives. The study is a necessarily brief and oversimplified account of the life-histories of the megalithic monuments in the region of Galicia (NW Iberia) between 569 and 1865 AD, paying particular attention to the variety of roles that they played throughout. Thus I aim to contribute to filling the research gap between their 'childhood' and their present state, which seem to be almost the only two moments of these monuments' lives hitherto considered. Furthermore, it is hoped that this case study may serve to illustrate the validity of this research strategy. Some wider implications of the approach for archaeology and heritage management shall also be outlined.

2. SOURCES AND METHODOLOGY

The resources and methodology used for this research have already been detailed elsewhere (Martinón-Torres 2001b: 25-32), therefore only a summary is presented here. In this case, only written sources have been utilised. Given the great variability of names used to refer to megaliths in different times and regions, the first step was the elaboration of a list with all the toponyms likely to be used for these monuments. The database of toponyms amounted to 134 entries, however, only a few will appear in this paper: *arca, anta, dolmen, mámoa, mama, mamula, meda, medorra, medoña,* and some derivatives. Once the list was completed, the search for those toponyms in historic books and documents began. A wide range of sources for the life-histories of megaliths was thus found and reviewed, the key of which are outlined below.

a) *Estate record books (6th-16th century):* these are the books in which medieval landlords used to keep record of the transactions regarding their properties. Leasings, buyings and sellings, wills, inheritances… all generated documents that were kept together, paying particular attention to the boundaries of the lands involved.

b) *Trial record of Vázquez de Orjas (1609 AD):* the origins of this book are to be found in a series of trials that took place in the early 17th century. It addresses the looting of hundreds of barrows by treasure hunters, in what was the most tremendous gold rush in the history of Galicia.

c) *Ensenada's Cadastre (1749):* these books result from a survey directed by Ensenada, an 18th-century Spanish minister who imposed a new tax based on patrimony. For this purpose, he needed a complete record of all civil and ecclesiastical properties, including the lands, with their exact location and boundaries.

d) *Books of history and geography (15th century – 1865):* looking for megaliths mentioned either as historical remains or as elements of the landscape, a review was conducted of all the books of geography and history referred to NW Iberia, from the first ones in the 15th century until the momentous date of 1865.

e) *Books of toponyms (19th century):* place names often provide information on the past of the places. However, place names change throughout time, which may entail the loss of those historical remembrances. Bearing this in mind, old books of toponyms were examined in search of references to places whose names might hint at megalithic monuments.

3. THE ROLES OF THE MONUMENTS DURING THEIR LIFE-HISTORIES

3.1. Territorial role

It is widely accepted that megaliths played a territorial role during prehistoric times. Conceived as elements which were highly visible in the landscape, the monuments *marked* the space where they were placed, and this idea has served as the basis for many studies of the spatial implications of the monuments within prehistoric societies (starting with Fleming 1972 and Renfrew 1973; 1976; then followed by many others). Whether this territorial role of the monuments has lasted with the monuments has seldom been studied. Only a few researchers have dealt with the role of megalithic monuments as land marks during historical periods (cf. for NW Iberia, Ferro 1952; Filgueira and García 1977; Criado and Grajal 1981; Pena 1991; Carneiro 1995; Martinón-Torres 2001a; 2001b).

Our account of the life-histories of the monuments starts in 569. In this year, an ecclesiastical council was organized in Braga, Portugal, with the main purpose of re-arranging the dioceses of the NW of the Iberian Peninsula. The new ecclesiastical provinces were defined very accurately, detailing the limits and boundaries of each particular diocese. The resulting document, known as *Parroquial Suevo* or *División de Teodomiro*, provides an account of the different parishes contained in each diocese, together with their boundaries. In order to establish these borderlines, references are made to old paths, hills, springs… and also to archaeological remains that serve as boundary markers. In particular, when the limits of a county are given, it is stated that the boundary '*pertransit ad Mamula de Gutilanes*' (Carneiro 1995: 299).

In this boundary that 'runs through the mound of Gutilanes' is the earliest known written reference to a Galician megalith playing a territorial role. However, from this moment onwards, the number of such references will not but increase remarkably. In medieval and early modern estate record books (6th - 16th centuries) we find, on the one hand, expressions such as *ad illam mamunam in prono ad Campellos, ad archa antiqua, per illas mamuas de Sancta Marina, ad illa mamoa der inter Ardilleiros et Eldar, per mammuam furatam, per arcam que est in monte super Vilarino, per illum lumbum inter ambas antas, per petras fitas, ad illam mamolam terrenam de Castrilu, per illas mamonas de Foranas de Vlar, ad alia arca pitrinia*…utlised to demarcate a given piece of land by making use of megalithic boundary markers.

Similarly, these sources include place names like *grangiam de Modorra, hereditatem quam dicunt Archas, Monte de Meda, ad montem qui dicitur Meda, strata usque ubi dicent Antas, grangiam de Archas, loco qui dicitur Arca, loco qui vocatur Mamoelas*… in which the monument seems to have become the visible icon giving rise to the name of the place where it stands.

Over 250 such references were found, being especially abundant between the 11th and the 13th centuries. In some cases, we can track many references to the very same megalithic landmarks which preserved their function throughout several centuries. This indicates that the territorial role of the megaliths was considerably important in medieval Galicia. Given their age, solidity and visibility, it seems that the monuments became territorial referents conventionally accepted and used in different districts. This is illustrated in the estate records from the monastery of San Esteban de Ribas de Sil: in 921, the King Ordoño III granted the monastery numerous properties. They appear limited by several landmarks, among them: '*ad mamola de Villare... et per illa petra scripta que est inter Faramontaos et Eiratella... et inde per Petra Fita, et inde per medium montium que vocitant Meta*' (Duro 1977: doc. 1). Subsequently, in later centuries, the granting of this holdings was to be corroborated by Alfonso IX, Ferdinand IV, Peter I, John I and John II... who again referred to those megalithic landmarks (docs. 11, 62, 76, 92 and 112). Just as the monuments lasted, so did their function.

Later on, in the 18th century, we again can find references to megalithic monuments as landmarks – now in Ensenada's Cadastre. For example, the boundary of the parish of San Miguel de Codesoso 'comes to the mámoa of Abrigadoiro... and then towards the North, up to the mámoa of Couso de Catarrán' (1036v). That of Santa María de las Puentes de García Rodríguez extends 'to the modoña de Cotillón... and from this to mama furada' (3356rv). However such references are not so frequent at this stage, and the only monuments playing territorial roles are normally those confined to less densely inhabited areas.

After that, in the 19th century, we only find references to monuments functioning as landmarks in the books of toponyms (Villarroel 1810; Madoz 1845-50). In these sources we find place names such as *lugar de Mámoa, lugar de Madorras, Santiago de la Medorra...* which actually relate to the one-time presence of monuments playing a somewhat territorial role. Nonetheless, it could be argued that the territorial value of the megaliths at this point is already vague: a toponym may be just a name inherited from the past, and in the 19th century these landmarks are no longer needed. Instead, the properties are normally surrounded by walls or hedges and illustrated in maps.

3.2. Symbolic role

Megaliths have also played a symbolic role during their life-histories. This becomes clear when they are alluded to as mysterious hiding places for non-existent treasures, as well as when they are involved in myths, legends and a variety of ritual activities. It should be noted that although 'symbolism' is overtly used here in a broad sense, the appropriation of monuments as ancestors' remains to found political claims is *not* considered as 'symbolic' but rather as an expression of the 'archaeological role' of the monuments (see next section).

It can be assumed that the monuments were already playing a symbolic role during the first centuries of the Middle Ages. In the medieval ecclesiastical councils of Arles (443-452), Tours (567), Nantes (658) and Toledo (681 and 693), claims are raised against heretical pagan rituals and cults of stones. Even though I have not been able to find any specific reference to megalithic monuments, I suppose that the cults of stones and other rituals would often take place at 'special features' in the landscape such as striking rock outcrops or ancient stone constructions – as still happens nowadays.

Nevertheless, the real outbreak of the symbolic role played by the monuments was to come in the 17th century. At this time, the priest Pedro Vázquez de Orjas came back from America, presumably knowing about the great treasures actually hidden and looted in some of the South American monuments. Following an extensive survey undertaken in 1603 in search of Galician monuments, the results of which are unfortunately lost, he persuaded the King Philip III that there were huge amounts of gold buried in the megaliths. Consequently, in 1606, Vázquez de Orjas was granted a royal franchise that allowed him to recover for the Treasury that gold supposedly preserved in the graves of the *gentiles galigrecos*. In return he would receive a commission.

As soon as the priest's activity began and the word spread, the gold rush erupted. Hundreds of peasants started their own excavations at different mounds, expecting to recover the precious goods before the gold would go to enlarge the Royal Treasury. As Vázquez de Orjas himself relates the episode,

'Many people, with little fear of God, Our Lord, and defying His Majesty the King – whose sole name should be enough to refrain them –, have been as bold as to have opened and open and dig and loot the aforementioned graves... and they hide what they find in some of them, thus scandalizing the Christian Republic.' (290r)

This episode is today known from the documentation resulting from the series of trials that ensued, preserved in the Archivo del Reino de Galicia as lawsuit No. 27219. The so-called 'Vázquez de Orjas affair' had been briefly cited in several publications (Murguía 1888: 98; 1901: 461; Martínez 1909; Blanco Freijeiro 1988: 41; Rodríguez Casal 1990: 53-57; 1991: 125-126; 1993: 55; 1997: 449; Pena Graña 1991: 34; Masset: 1993; Aparicio Casado: 1999). However, it was not thoroughly read and transcribed until recently (Martinón-Torres 2001b; 2002a). Nowadays this legal case file can be studied as an invaluable source for the history of Galician archaeology. It reports severe accusations, premeditated deceit, strict judgements, arguments regarding ownership, descriptions of monuments being destroyed... together with substantial insinuations of the symbolic role of the monuments.

The fact that the barrows were looted in the hunt for illusory gold that had never been there demonstrates the symbolic role of the monuments. The power of the monuments must have been immense. According to this source, some peasants carried weapons in order to face the fear. Others, instead, would be 'armed' with holy water and seek advise from wizards. No one knew exactly what these mounds were; however, almost everyone believed that they held treasure. In addition, most of the treasure is referred purely as gold, with no indication of the particular goods found. This allusion to unspecified gold treasure is commonplace in Galician popular myths, even today (Llinares García 1991: 30). Furthermore, throughout the trial record, in those cases where the allegedly found items are mentioned, suspects and witnesses mention such goods as, for example, 'a gold saint that weighed three pounds and a half' (221r), 'a small gold chest' (224r), 'a gold cat' (318v) or 'a gold plough' (322r)... Moreover, it is reported that, due to the presence of gold, there are cows whose colours change (317v-318r) and sporadic apparitions in of chicks and chickens (317v). This again underlines the more mythical than material nature of such treasure.

The symbolic function of the monuments in 17th-century NW Iberia may also be gleaned from the account of some other events that supposedly took place in the surroundings of some barrows. Martínez Salazar (1909: 218-219) had already noted the relevance of these testimonies which are translated here:

'Hilario Alonso had found there a woman unkempt and dressed in brown-coloured pelt and with her hair loose, and this at night... And she was holding some hairs in her hand, and had asked him what he deemed better, either what she was holding in her hand or herself. To what he answered that herself... And thus she had sent him to excavate at the hill of the barrow of Segade, because he would find there a treasure.'

'[The witness declares that] the aforementioned woman had called him at dusk and asked him what he considered as better, either herself or some wires that she had tied in her hands, which looked like gold... And that he answered that he considered herself as better, and the aforementioned told him "Blessed the mother who gave birth to you". And [declares] that the woman was dark and ugly and talked through her nose.'

All in all, the Vázquez de Orjas affair suggests that the symbolic role of the megaliths probably was the most important one at the beginnings of the 17th century. As indicated above, this significance would have certainly been operating in the past, however at this moment – due to the priest's claims –, it appears intensified. The monuments were, above all, hiding places for wonderful treasure, regardless of their origins or other functions. This situation was to change only during the Enlightenment.

In the 18th century, the new ideas of the European Enlightenment started to spread within the erudite spheres. The Enlightenment meant putting 'Reason' on a pedestal. 'Reason' was the light that enabled knowledge and correction. Nothing could be accepted unless it was subjected to the new rationality: neither superstition nor credulity nor other traditional obstacles to progress. On these grounds, the first criticisms arise of many beliefs that had seldom or never been challenged before – including those involving megaliths.

Father Sarmiento was one the main supporters of this modern way of thinking. In his writings, we often find emphatic criticisms of common peasants, who showed 'the most fatuous credibility that one could ever imagine' (Sarmiento 1996: 67v). According to him, the search of wealth in mounds was the activity of 'the greedy, the ignorant and the idle person' (Sarmiento 1996: 66v), for no gold treasure could be found in any of such monuments. Subsequently, Sarmiento and other scholars of the Enlightenment started a crusade for the education of the lower classes. The beliefs about treasures hidden in megaliths and other myths related to ancient ruins are still alive in some Galician villages. Sometimes they are still believed to be true, however they are quickly disappearing under the shadow cast by the modern rational knowledge (Llinares 1990; 1991; Alonso 1998; Aparicio 1999). This symbolic role of the monuments is thus progressively decreasing, and we have to see the Enlightenment as the new outlook behind this change.

3.3. Archaeological role

Let us now address the archaeological role played by the monuments during their life-histories. Nowadays it appears obvious that megalithic monuments are ancient and that, as such, they may serve as sources of information about the past. However, this idea has not always been recognised, and indeed its historical origins may be dated with a certain precision.

Significantly, no references to megaliths were made in any of the books of history written about Galicia from the 15th to the 17th century (Martinón-Torres 2001b). The first Galician historical writings showed a strong apologist bias and aimed at defending Galician idiosyncrasy. (Barreiro Fernández 1988). They re-created the past and made a fairly indiscriminate use of sources and historical episodes in order to fulfil their particular aims. Nonetheless, it seems that megaliths were not seen as an important element of the past which could be used to illustrate the allegedly historic Galician character.

It was only during the 18th-century Enlightenment that megaliths started to appear in historical productions. Here the pioneering role of Father Sarmiento must be considered (cf. Martinón-Torres 2004). He claimed that the monuments were not the product of legendary beings and posed an alternative explanation. According to him, the mámoas were ancient constructions housing the funerary urns of the Romans. Even though he failed to identify the actual builders of the monuments, he emphasised the fact that the megaliths were a human creation from the past. This has to be seen as the first step on the way to realise the archaeological role of the monuments. For the first time, Sarmiento observed the monuments with aspirations of objectivity. He provided thorough descriptions of the barrows and raised hypotheses about how they were constructed. Moreover, he considered that the study of the monuments would allow scholars to improve their knowledge of 'geography, antiquity and history, and thus overcome the lack of much unknown [information] from ancient authors that has not been preserved' (Sarmiento 1950: 74). In other words, according to him, despite their inability to reveal fabulous treasures, the monuments were still worth exploration, but rather in search of clues to understand the past. This sowed the seed of an approach towards megaliths which is still preponderant in the current academic world.

Subsequent to Sarmiento's advocation of the archaeological role of megaliths, 19th-century historians of Galicia paid an increasing attention to the monuments when reconstructing the past. At this time, books of history were strongly influenced by nationalistic ideologies. Galician intellectuals were fighting to defend the individuality of NW Iberia against the Spanish totalitarism, and any ideological weapon was of use in this aim. In this context, the hypothesis of a distinct prehistoric celtic race living and surviving in some regions of Europe – including Galicia – was widely accepted and adopted as a part of the national character. Thus the history of Galicia had to be re-written, this time as a national history of the 'Celtic' Galicia. The 'Celtic myth' (Barreiro 1986; 1988; Pereira 2000) was hence established, which would draw expressly on megalithic monuments.

Nineteenth-century Galician historians usually thought megaliths to have been built by the Celts (cf. Martinón-Torres 2000a). Therefore, they failed again to ascribe them to the correct period, which is understandable if we consider the ideological constraints and the lack of archaeological excavations at that time. However, and more importantly, they emphasised the archaeological role of the monuments to such an extent that still nowadays this is considered as the main – if not the only – value of the megaliths.

In 1838, Verea y Aguiar published the first volume of his *Historia de Galicia*, where he interpreted megaliths as the tombs of the Celtic tribes and encouraged the preservation and study. Soon after this, in 1849 and 1850, Martínez de Padín's work was published. This work, which was explicitly addressed 'to the historian, the archaeologist and the man of letters, as well as to those dedicated to sciences' (Martínez de Padín 1849: 17), dealt explicitly with the monuments. Martínez de Padín described the megalithic constructions, classified them typologically, and tried to interpret their function, aided by foreign literature on the topic. The megalithic monuments were remains from the past and thus they were approached as such, regardless of other possible values and despite methodological difficulties.

The definitive acme of the archaeological significance of the megaliths took place in 1865. In this year, two of the foremost histories of Galicia were published, which meant a revolution not only in the subsequent writing of history but also in the way that monuments were dealt with. On the one hand, Benito Vicetto's (1865) *Historia de Galicia* devoted several pages to what he called '*Celtic antiquities*'. He was strongly conditioned by his love to his motherland and his vivid imagination, therefore his work lacked academic standards. Nevertheless, he was able to show the monuments displaying their archaeological function. Considering them as the tombs of their 'illustrious' ancestors, Vicetto described them in detail, again offering typologies and raising hypotheses as to their origins. Furthermore, he tried to reconstruct the ancient funerary rituals, although here he drew more from his imagination than from real archaeological data. On the other hand, Manuel Murguía's (1865) work was so influential regarding the later life-histories of megaliths that its influence is still noticeable today.

Murguía was one of the first historians of Galicia who questioned the accuracy of ancient writers. Accordingly, he tried to find alternative ways of contrast the information given in historical sources. He found in archaeology the best method for this purpose. Fully acquainted with the archaeological literature published in Europe, Murguía developed an increasing interest in this field. His work is full of enthusiasm for the archaeology as a discipline, even though he himself would never undertake an archaeological excavation. He presented the monuments, above all, as containers of information about his ancestors. In various fragments of his *Historia de Galicia,* megaliths are thoroughly described and scrutinised, as well as classified in formal typologies. They are interpreted with reference to various burial rituals, and their origins are suggested drawing from contemporary ethnology and diffusionist theories. Overall, the monuments were sources of information, 'open books in which the historian reads even clearer than in Greek and Roman authors' (Murguía 1865: 395).

Murguía's contribution to the development of archaeology in Galicia and his influence in the way that monuments are nowadays approached have been discussed elsewhere (Martinón-Torres 2000). However, the above should suffice to demonstrate his relevance regarding the biographies of monuments. As he considered the megaliths as the tombs of the idealized Celts, it could be argued that the monuments still preserve some of their symbolic power in the 19th century. Furthermore, he refers to treasure hunters still operating while he writes. Nevertheless, the common approach to the monuments subsequent to Murguía's *Historia de Galicia* shall always emphasise their archaeological role. Most of the current archaeological excavations aim at dating the monuments and enhancing our knowledge of prehistoric societies. In other words, they only consider their archaeological value. This has to be seen as the result of Murguía's approach.

4. SUMMARY AND INTERPRETATION

The investigation of the written references to megaliths from 569 to 1865 AD allows an overview of the evolution of the main functions played by Galician megaliths during this period of their life-histories. An attempt to summarise this evolution graphically is presented in Figure 1, although it must be stressed that the nature of the diagram is purely qualitative and illustrative.

As we have seen, the territorial role seems to have been the major value of the monuments during the Middle Ages. The mounds could have been playing this role since prehistoric times, and maybe this was one of the main reasons for their preservation over the centuries (cf. Martinón-Torres 2001a). In medieval times, many people would almost certainly feel their symbolic power, and, in fact, perhaps the idea of a 'symbolic protection' from the ancestors was behind their use as boundary markers.

However, it is not until the 17th century, when Vázquez de Orjas spreads his idea of the monuments' treasure, that the symbolic role of the megaliths is fully valued. Simulta-

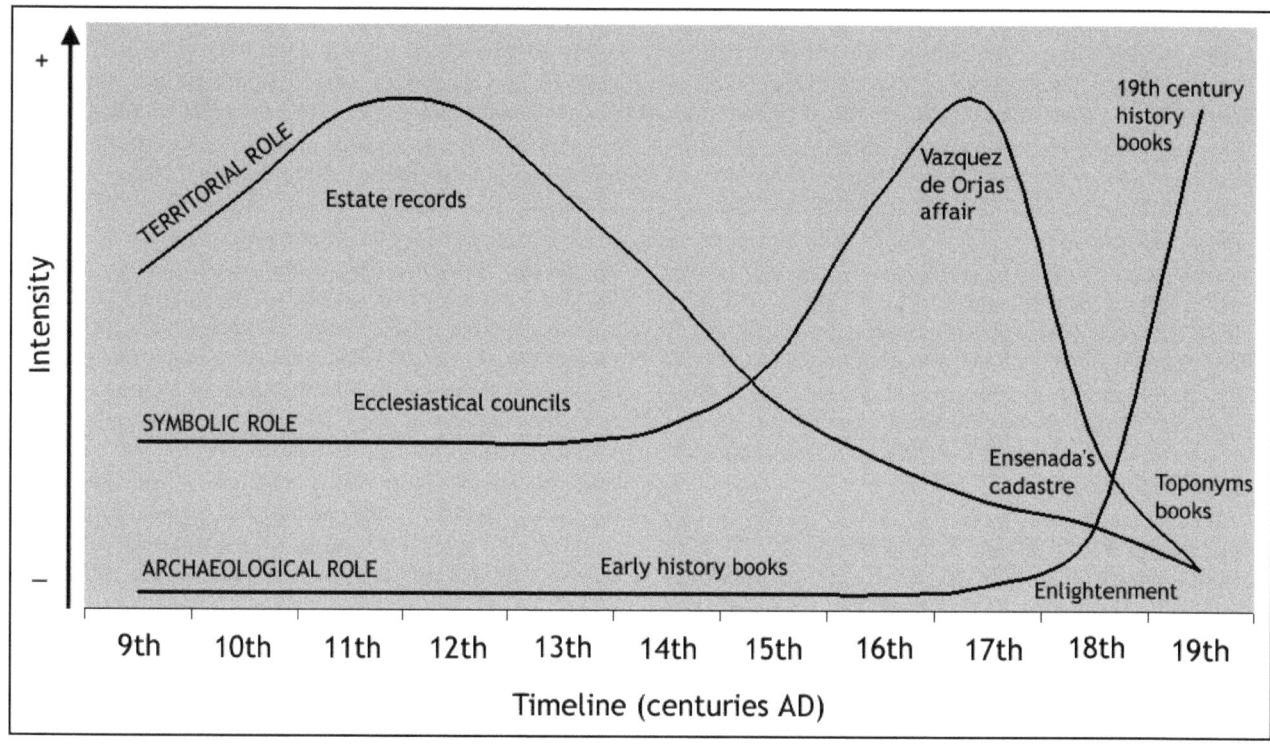

Figure 1. Diachronic sketch of the intensity of three main roles played by the monuments during their later life-histories, with indication of the main sources and events referred to in the text. Note how the archaeological role only rises as both territorial and symbolic roles decline.

neously, as Galician peasants embark on the task of recovering legendary treasures, the territorial role of the monuments seems to decline. In fact, as explained above, the number of references to megaliths as landmarks decreases during the 18th century and almost disappears in the 19th. While the evolving technical resources would make the construction of walls around the lands easier, the symbolic power of the monuments would become more important. Indeed, stones from destroyed megaliths could often be used to make those walls. Many of the monuments found in medieval estate record books were probably looted in the 17th century, and thus very scarce remains are left for the present-day archaeologist, except for written references.

Finally, and significantly, the monuments do not display their archaeological role in full until the decease of both their territorial and symbolic values. Indeed, the early supporters of this 'informative' function of the megaliths are scholars who neither need the landmarks nor believe in fantastic treasures. At the time of Vázquez de Orjas's affair, most of the inhabitants of Galicia would have known about the existence of these ancient structures. However, only a few of them just mention that they are *'the tombs of gentiles galigrecos'* and the monuments do not appear at all in the books of history of the time. Only since the Enlightenment, once popular beliefs start to be systematically condemned, and when megaliths are no longer the landmarks that they used to be, do the monuments begin to display their archaeological value. Since this period, the archaeological value of the monuments has been constantly reinforced, this being mainly due to authors like Father Sarmiento and Manuel Murguía. They can be considered as largely the responsible for the hegemony of archaeology over other approaches to megaliths.

5. CONCLUSION

This account of the life-histories of megaliths in NW Iberia has necessarily been brief and incomplete. Firstly, because the chronological lapse itself is limited; only one period of the monuments' lives was explored. Secondly, because only literary sources were used – the author strongly believes that the study of the life-histories of monuments should be complemented by other approaches such as archaeological excavation. Thirdly, this study is limited since, as I intended to provide a broad diachronic picture, some of the specific receptions of the monuments at different times have been overlooked, as well as other issues such as the physical changes of the monuments resulting from their evolving functions.

As soon as we broaden our range of sources and perspectives, more roles and meanings of the megaliths can be identified. The three broad classes characterised above – i.e. territorial, symbolic and archaeological – could be broken down into many different subcategories, and conversely there may be historical receptions of the monuments which do not fit comfortably in any of them. Furthermore, as noted above, these roles overlap, and just as the role of the monuments as boundary markers may have symbolic connotations, so does the use of the monuments in historical or archaeological narratives. As a counterpoint to this study, Holtorf's (2000-2) reconstruction of the monuments' life-histories in Mecklenburg-Vorpommern (Germany) did not attempt any assessment of the relative weights of different roles, or an evolutionary interpretation, but the resulting picture is in turn more comprehensive and colourful. Even though archaeologists and heritage managers are usually the most established individuals dealing with megaliths in the present day, the monuments are more than mere suppliers of historical knowledge and heritage tourism resources. The variety of later receptions is crucial insofar as these may lead to different approaches to the monuments and, hence, they affect the monuments' lives. This happened in the past as well as in the present. For example, some may wish to excavate the megaliths through archaeological means, whereas others may prefer keeping them for ritual purposes, and others may just want to eliminate them in the wake of development.

Primarily, this paper has tried to show the value of studying the monuments' life-histories. Megaliths were conceived, most likely, not only for the present but also with a view to the future (e.g. Sherrat 1995; Holtorf 1996; 2000-02). We cannot fail to notice the fact that they have lasted and interacted with different societies of various ages. Thus the monuments have to be studied as long-lasting entities. Accordingly, it is hoped that archaeological excavations shall take more into account all the episodes of megaliths' lives (e.g. Holtorf 2001). However, this study has posed an additional theme: the diversity of the megaliths' roles and, hence, the variety of current approaches to them. It has been shown that the preponderance of the archaeological role of the monuments is a construct of our specific sociohistorical context – just one dimension of the megaliths' lives. The monuments are sources of information about the past, but also collective burials, boundary markers and icons of identity. In addition, they are, and have been, houses of mythical beings, raw material for stoneworkers, inspiration for photographers, painters and other artists. Moreover they are, and may have been, hidden places for treasure, pleasant stops for walkers, mines for antiquarians and looters, basis for intricate archaeoastronomic formulations and lively debates as to heritage management, excuses for the invention of traditions, legitimation for political postures... The list is endless.

As archaeologists, the law normally privileges our approach towards, and own interests in, the monuments. However, peasants, artists, thinkers, stoneworkers, travellers, judges, historians, politicians, druids, constructors... have also dealt and deal with megaliths, thus interacting in their life-histories. Whose approach is the most authentic or legitimate? This study has demonstrated that the receptions and uses of the monuments depend very much on the changing social and cultural contexts. Whilst far from advocating that 'anything goes' in the management of archaeological sites, I belive that this may well prove to be another instance where history will teach us that today's truths are tomorrow's myths. As the monuments' lives continue, perhaps those of us in a privileged position to deal with them should be more flexible and take into account the voice of those whose views are traditionally dismissed.

Acknowledgements

I am deeply grateful to Antón A. Rodríguez Casal for his directions in locating the sources and for his permanent encouragement. I am also indebted to Sarah McCarthy and Renata Peters for correcting my use of English. During the various stages of this research, I enjoyed postgraduate scholarships from the Secretary of Research and Development of the Xunta de Galicia (Spain), Pedro Barrié de la Maza Foundation, The British Council, and Caixanova Foundation. The support of these institutions is thankfully acknowledged.

Author's Address

Mario MARTINÓN-TORRES
Institute of Archaeology
University College London
31-34 Gordon Square
London WC1H 0PY, UNITED KINGDOM
Email: m.martinon-torres@ucl.ac.uk

Bibliography

ALONSO ROMERO, F., 1998, Las mouras constructoras de megalitos: Estudio comparativo del folklore gallego con el de otras comunidades europeas. *Anuario Brigantino* 21, pp. 11-28.

APARICIO CASADO, B., 1999, *Mouras, serpientes, tesoros y otros encantos. Mitología popular gallega*. Sada: Ediciós do Castro.

BARREIRO FERNÁNDEZ, X.R., 1986, A recriación do mito celta. *A Nosa Terra. A Nosa Cultura*, Extra No. 7, pp. 27-29.

BARREIRO FERNÁNDEZ, X.R., 1988, La historia de la Historia. Aproximación a una historiografía gallega (siglos XVI-XIX). In *IV Xornadas de Historia de Galicia. Historiografía gallega*, edited by X. Castro and J. de Juana. Ourense: Diputación Provincial de Ourense, pp. 15-80.

BENDER, B., 1993, Stonehenge – Contested Landscapes (Medieval to Present-Day). In *Landscapes. Politics and Perspectives*, edited by B. Benders. Providence and Oxford: Berg, pp. 245-279.

BLANCO FREIJEIRO, A., 1988, *Los primeros españoles*. Madrid: Historia 16.

BRADLEY, R., 1984, Studying monuments. In *Neolithic Studies: A Review of Some Current Research*, edited by R. Bradley and J. Gardiner. Oxford: British Archaeological Reports, BS, pp. 61-66.

BRADLEY, R., 1993, *Altering the Earth. The Origins of Monuments in Britain and Continental Europe*. Edinburgh: Society of Antiquaries of Scotland.

BRADLEY, R., 1996, Ancestors and identity in the later prehistory of Atlantic Scotland: the reuse and reinvention of Neolithic monuments and material culture. *World Archaeology* 28(2), pp. 231-243.

BRADLEY, R., 2000, Vera Collum and the excavation of a 'Roman' megalithic tomb. *Antiquity* 70, pp. 39-43.

BRADLEY, R., & WILLIAMS, H. (eds), 1998, *The Past in the Past: The Reuse of Ancient Monuments*. (*World Archaeology* 30(1)).

CAAMAÑO GESTO, J.M., & CRIADO BOADO, F., 1991-2, La medorra de Fanegas (Sobrado dos Monxes, A Coruña). Un monumento megalítico reutilizado en época romana. *Brigantium* 7, pp. 7-89.

CARNEIRO REY, J.A., 1995, El fenómeno tumular en Narón: análisis de localización. *Estudios Mindonienses* 11, pp. 293-362.

CHIPPINDALE, C., 1994, *Stonehenge Complete* (rev. edn.). London: Thames and Hudson.

CRIADO BOADO, F., & GRAJAL, M., 1981, Relación entre la distribución de mámoas y el medio físico en la zona de Sobrado-Curtis. *Brigantium* 2, pp. 7-26.

DANIEL, G., 1972, *Megalihts in History*. London: Thames and Hudson.

DURO PEÑA, E., 1977, *El monasterio de San Esteban de Ribas de Sil*. Ourense: Instituto de Estudios Orensanos Padre Feijoó.

FERRO COUSELO, J., 1952, *Los petroglifos de término y las insculturas rupestres de Galicia*. Ourense: Talleres gráficos de Miguel López Elizalde.

FILGUEIRA VALVERDE, J., & GARCÍA ALÉN, A., 1977, Inventario de monumentos megalíticos en la provincia de Pontevedra. *El Museo de Pontevedra* 31, pp. 49-130.

FLEMING, G., 1973, Tombs for the Living. *MAN* 8, pp. 177-193.

HINGLEY, R., 1996, Ancestors and identity in the later prehistory of Atlantic Scotland: the reuse and reinvention of Neolithic monuments and material culture. *World Archaeology* 28(2), pp. 231-243.

HOLTORF, C.J., 1996, Towards a chrono*logy* of megaliths: understanding monumental time and cultural memory. *Journal of European Archaeology* 4, pp. 119-152.

HOLTORF, C.J., 1997, Beyond Chronographies of Megaliths: Understanding Monumental Time and Cultural Memory. In *O Neolítico Atlántico e as orixes do Megalitismo*, edited by A. A. Rodríguez Casal. Santiago de Compostela: Universidade de Santiago de Compostela, pp. 101-114.

HOLTORF, C.J., 1998, The life-histories of megaliths in Mecklenburgh-Vorpommern (Germany). *World Archaeolgy* 30(1), pp. 23-38.

HOLTORF, C.J., 2001, A história da vida de um monumento pré-historico. Trabalho de Pesquisa no Monte da Igreja, Freg. Torre de Coelheiros. *A Cidade de Évora* (2nd series) 4, pp. 57-82.

HOLTORF, C.J., 2000-2, Monumental Past:. The Life-histories of Megalithic Monuments in Mecklenburg-Vorpommern (Germany). Electronic monograph. University of Toronto: Centre for Instructional Technology Development. https://tspace.library.utoronto.ca/citd/holtorf/index.html

LLINARES GARCÍA, M., 1990, *Mouros, ánimas, demonios: El imaginario popular gallego*. Madrid: Akal.

LLINARES GARCÍA, M., 1991, *Os mouros no imaxinario popular*. Santiago de Compostela: El Correo Gallego.

LOWENTHAL, D., 1999, *The Past is a Foreign Country* (1st edn. 1985). Cambridge: Cambridge University Press.

MADOZ, P., 1845-50, *Diccionario Geográfico-Estadístico-Histórico de España y sus posesiones de Ultramar. Galicia*. Facsímile edited by J.J. Vega González. Santiago de Compostela: Libros Galicia, 6 vols.

MARTÍNEZ DE PADÍN, L., 1849-50, *Historia política, religiosa y descriptiva de Galicia*, 2 vols. Madrid: Establecimiento tipográfico de A. Vicente.

MARTÍNEZ SALAZAR, M., 1909, Sobre apertura de mámoas a principios del siglo XVII. *Boletín de la Real Academia Gallega* 3, pp. 26ff.

MARTINÓN-TORRES, M., 2000a, Análisis del 'megalitismo céltico' en la Galicia del siglo XIX. *Gallaecia* 19, pp. 289-307.

MARTINÓN-TORRES, M., 2000b, Murguía e a arqueoloxía galega. *Boletín da Real Academia Galega* 361, pp. 221-244.

MARTINÓN-TORRES, M., 2001a, Los megalitos de término. Crónica del valor territorial de los monumentos megalíticos a partir de las fuentes escritas. *Trabajos de Prehistoria* 58(1), pp. 95-108.

MARTINÓN-TORRES, M., 2001b, *Os monumentos megalíticos despois do megalitismo. Arqueoloxía e historia dos megalitos galegos a través das fontes escritas (s.VI – s.XIX)*. Valga: Concello de Valga.

MARTINÓN-TORRES, M., in press, El Padre Sarmiento y el descubrimiento del megalitismo gallego como fenómeno de interés arqueológico. *Cuadernos de Estudios Gallegos* 116.

MARTINÓN-TORRES, M., 2002a, Defying God and the King: a 17th-century gold rush for 'megalithic treasure'. *Public Archaeology* 2(4), pp. 220-235

MARTINÓN-TORRES, M., 2002b, Review of: Cornelius J. Holtorf: Monumental Past: The Life-histories of Megalithic Monuments in Mecklenburg-Vorpommern (Germany). *Papers from the Institute of Archaeology (PIA)* 13, pp. 131-137.

MARTINÓN-TORRES, M., & RODRÍGUEZ CASAL, A. 2000, Aspectos historiográficos del megalitismo gallego: de la documentación medieval al siglo XIX. In *Actas do III Congresso de Arqueologia Peninsular*, vol. 3: *Neolitização e Megalitismo da Península Ibérica*, edited by V. Oliveira Jorge. Porto: ADECAP, pp. 303-319.

MASSET, C., 1993, *Les dolmens. Sociétés néolíthiques et pratiques funéraires*. Paris: Errance.

MURGUÍA, M., 1865, *Historia de Galicia*, vol. 1 (1st edn.). Lugo: Imprenta de Soto Freire.

MURGUÍA, M., 1888, Galicia. In *España. Sus monumentos y artes. Su naturaleza é Historia*. Barcelona: Daniel Cortezo.

MURGUÍA, M., 1901, *Historia de Galicia*, vol. 1 (2nd rev. edn.). A Coruña: Librería de D. Eugenio Carré.

PATTON, M., 1996, La Hougue Bie à Jersey: transformation d'un monument du Néolitique à nos jours. *Bulletin de la Société Préhistorique Française* 93, pp. 298-300.

PENA GRAÑA, A., 1991, *Narón, un concello con historia de seu*. Narón: Servicio Sociopedagóxico Municipal.

PEREIRA GONZÁLEZ, F., 2000, O mito celta na historia. *Gallaecia* 19, pp. 311-334.

RENFREW, C., 1973, *Before Civilization. The Radiocarbon Revolution and Prehistoric Europe*. Harmondsworth: Penguin.

RENFREW, C., 1976, Megaliths, Territories and Populations. In *Acculturation and Continuity in Atlantic Europe*, edited by S. J. de Laet. Dissertationes Archaeologicae Gandenses XVI. Brugge: De Tempel, pp. 298-320.

RODRÍGUEZ CASAL, A.A., 1990, *O Megalitismo. A primeira arquitectura monumental de Galicia*. Santiago de Compostela: Universidade de Santiago de Compostela.

RODRÍGUEZ CASAL, A.A., 1991, El megalitismo gallego: la documentación arqueográfica. In *Galicia.Historia*, vol 3: *Prehistoria. Historia Antigua*, edited by J.M. Vázquez Varela and F. Acuña Castroviejo. A Coruña: Hércules.

RODRÍGUEZ CASAL, A.A., 1993, Análise historiográfica do megalitismo galego. In *Galicia e a Historiografía*, edited by J.G. Beramendi. Santiago de Compostela: Tórculo, pp. 53-71.

RODRÍGUEZ CASAL, A.A., 1997, Neolítico e Megalitismo en Galicia. In *O Neolítico Atlántico e as orixes do Megalitismo*, edited by A.A. Rodríguez Casal. Santiago de Compostela: Universidade de Santiago de Compostela, pp. 447-462.

SARMIENTO, M., 1950, *Viaje a Galicia (1754-55)*. Anejo 3 de *Cuaderno de Estudios Gallegos*. Santiago de Compostela: Instituto Padre Sarmiento de Estudios Gallegos.

SARMIENTO, M., 1996, *Escritos geográficos*. Santiago de Compostela: Xunta de Galicia, Consellería de Cultura.

SHERRATT, A., 1995, Instruments of conversion? The role of megaliths in the Mesolithic/Neolithic transition in North-West Europe. *Oxford Journal of Archaeology* 14(3), pp. 245-260.

VEREA Y AGUIAR, J., 1838, *Historia de Galicia. Primera Parte*. Ferrol: Imprenta de D. Nicasio Taxonera.

VICETTO, B., 1865, *Historia de Galicia*. Ferrol: Establecmiento tipográfico de Nicasio Taxonera.

VILLARROEL, J. de, 1810, Diccionario Nomenclator de las ciudades, villas, aldeas, caserías, cotos, ventas, castillos, y prioratos de todo el Reyno de Galicia. Santiago de Compostela: Imprenta de D. Juan Francisco Montero.

RESEARCH ON THE MEGALITHIC CULTURE OF GALICIA (NW IBERIAN PENINSULA) DURING THE LAST CENTURY

Antón A. RODRÍGUEZ CASAL

Abstract: Taking the most recent research undertaken with new methodologies as a starting point, this paper addresses the current state of our knowledge about the megalithic culture in Galicia (NW Iberian Peninsula). An emphasis is put on the historical evolution of the archaeological thought throughout the 20th century and on the research questions open for the future. It also presents an interdisciplinary research project carried out by a team of edafologists, geologists and archaeologists. Taking one region of the interior of Galicia as a case study, we analyse the relationship of soils and geological substrate with barrows and megaliths. The conclusions of this study lead us to challenge certain theories hitherto accepted which need a new reappraisal.

Resumé : En tenant compte des découvertes les plus récentes et des méthodologies actuelles, on présente l'état actuel de nos connaissances sur le mégalithisme en Galice (NW de la Péninsule Ibérique) tout en remarquant le sujet de l'évolution historique de la pensée archéologique tout au long du XXe siècle. A partir d'une recherche systématique menée sur place par une équipe interdisciplinaire avec des édaphologues, géologues et archéologues on analyse les rapports entre les sols et le substrat géologique, d'une part, et les tumulus et mégalithes dans une région de l'intérieur de la Galice. On met en question certaines théories admises généralement jusqu'à présent.

INTRODUCTION

One of the main features of the megalithic complex in Galicia, one of the Atlantic finisterrae, is given by the geographic distribution of the monuments all across the country (Fig. 1). Currently there are more than 5000 barrows documented. This gave rise to Manuel Murguía's statement in his *Historia de Galicia* (1st edition of 1865): "there is no uncultivated field in Galicia where the skilled eyes cannot perceive the big or small *mámoa*". The same idea would afterwards be expressed by Florentino López Cuevillas, who wrote that "Galicia and Northern Portugal up to the Duero river offer, in fact, and with respect to the surface of the region, a dolmenic density which is superior to any other Hispanic country" (LÓPEZ CUEVILLAS, 1973, p. 54). Only considering authors such as Manuel Murguía, especially his invaluable weight as a historian, his impassioned interest in archaeology and his pioneer role in the evolution of the studies of megaliths, can we understand the turn experimented by the archaeological research in Galicia at the beginnings of the century (MARTINÓN-TORRES 2000, p. 222; 2001, p. 160; this volume). In this sense, as we phrased it in a recent paper, "in the years following the publication of his *Historia de Galicia* we already find books which pay much attention to the megalithic culture. These pieces of work have to be understood as developments of an approach that Murguía himself started. Indeed current specialists just take steps – shorter or longer – on this same path" (MARTINÓN-TORRES & RODRÍGUEZ CASAL, 2000: 316).

1. RESEARCH DURING THE FIRST QUARTER OF THE 20TH CENTURY: FROM MURGUÍA TO "IMPRESIONES DE UN VIAJE PREHISTÓRICO POR GALICIA"

The start of the new century coincided with the publication of the 2nd edition of M. Murguía's *Historia de Galicia*, which showed a distinctively nineteenth-century understanding of history, but also introduced new approaches and a significant interest in the conservation of archaeological heritage. After two decades, again the state of affairs would change substantially, if not radically. Here we may mention authors such as N. Alberg, with the new methodological orientation exhibited in his *La Civilisation Enéolithique en la Péninsule Ibérique* (1920) and, above all, the publication in 1923 of the first sound compilation of Galician Prehistory, that is *Impresiones de un viaje prehistórico por Galicia*, by the German prehistorian Hugo Obermaier. This book exemplarily organizes all the data available at that time, collecting a diverse series of notes, descriptions and catalogues previously published by Murguía, Vázquez Núñez, Díaz Sanjurjo, Amor Meilán, Rodríguez Gallego, Fidel Pita, García de la Riega, Álvarez Carballido or Saralegui y Medina, among others.

Undoubtedly, in the context of the diffusionist theories of the time, Obermaier's work means a breakthrough and makes the date of 1923 an actual "annus mirabilis" in Galician historiography (FERNÁNDEZ IBÁÑEZ & FÁBREGAS, 1996, p. 120). Particularly notable are his ideas as to the possibility of contacts between megalith builders from the northwest and the south of the Iberian Peninsula. Furthermore, this author would catapult later studies by such relevant authors as Federico Maciñeira, Georg and Vera Leisner or Florentino López Cuevillas.

2. FROM THE TWENTIES TO THE SIXTIES: THE ENORMOUS WORK OF THE "CLASSIC AUTHORS"

Besides other minor contributions, this period was characterised by the studies of four outstanding figures, each of them with their particular personality. They would mean a new turn in the research on megaliths of the first half of the last century: Federico Maciñeira Pardo de

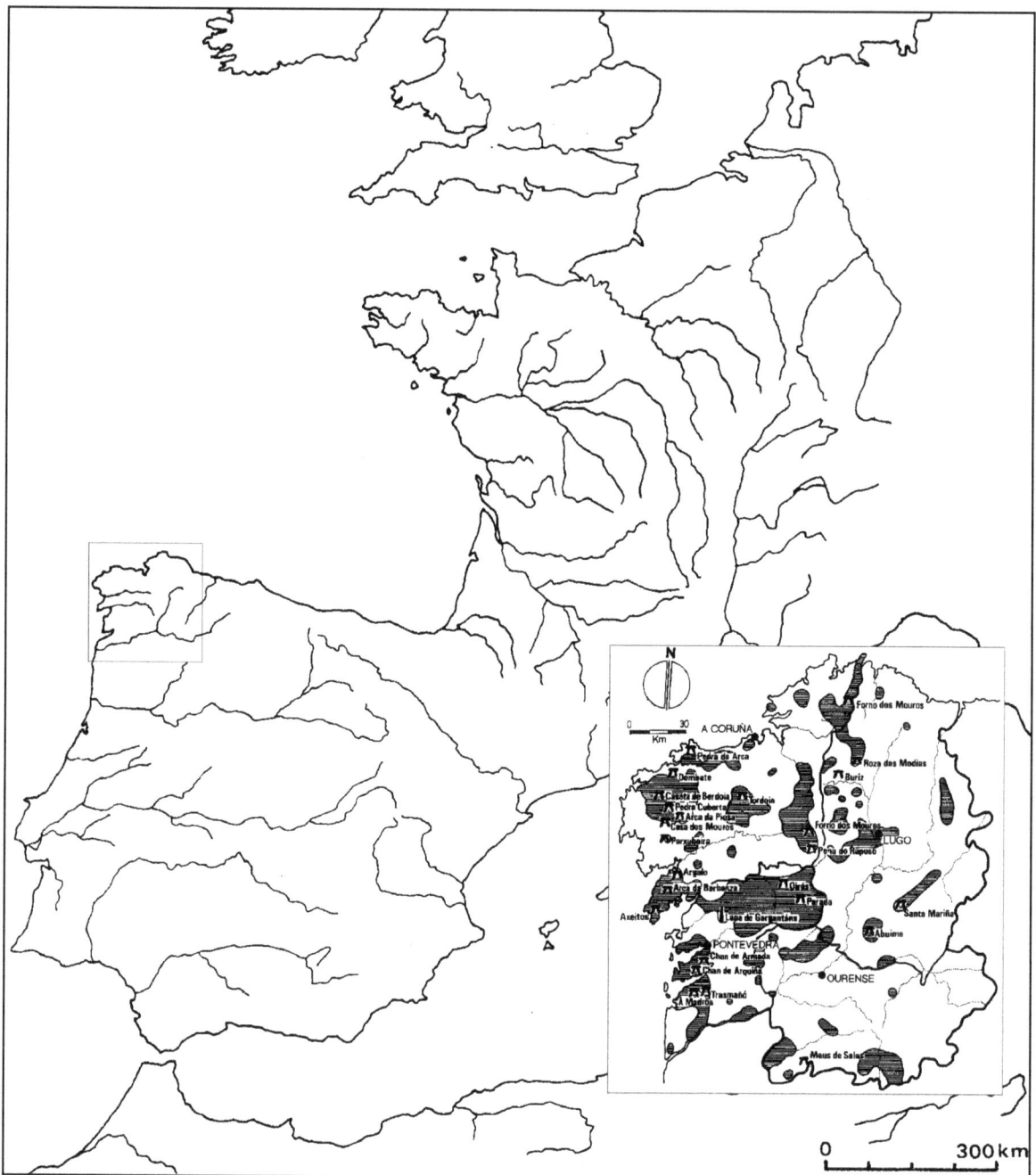

Figure 1. Galicia in the European Atlantic regions, with a detailed map of the megalithic distribution (1990).

Lama, the Leisners and Florentino López Cuevillas. The first of them embarked on a very thorough survey of the northern regions of Galicia. His work yielded several inventories with more than 300 megaliths in the districts of Bares, Sierra Faladoira and the higher and medium lands of the Eume river basin (MACIÑEIRA, 1929, 1935, 1943-1944), where he appears specifically interested in the relationship between barrows and old paths.

Besides providing fieldwork reports and inventories, Maciñeira related his finds to those from other regions from a diffusionist standpoint, and he also dealt with the Bell Beaker culture. The main conclusions of his research were expounded in his fundamental work, *Bares, Puerto hispánico de la primitiva navegación occidental*, published in 1947.

Just as Maciñeira is an essential reference for the study of the megalithic culture of northern Galicia, so is Florentino López Cuevillas to be commended as the person who gave the definitive boost to Galician archaeology. Unquestionably, this is the figure who best represents the philosophy of the Generation *Nós* and the Seminario de Estudos Galegos – even though the latter institution would stop its activity during the Spanish Civil War.

Cuevillas's approach to the megalithic culture was manifold. To start with, he undertook notable fieldwork in an attempt to reconstruct the original map of the megalithic distribution in the NW. In addition, he carried out diverse studies of archaeological materials held in museums and collections. This enabled him to address the various issues embraced by the megalithic culture from a palaeodemographic and palaeoeconomic point of view, as he himself illustrated in diverse scientific meetings and many publications. Articles such as "Os Oestrimnios, os Saefes e a ofiolatría en Galicia" (1929), (with Fermín Bouza Brey), "La Cultura megalítica del NW. peninsular" (1948), "Caracteres de la cultura megalítica del Noroeste peninsular (1953) or "La época megalítica en el noroeste de la Península" (1959) should be considered as classic pieces of work. His input in the study of Galician prehistory in general, and of the megalithic culture in particular, was extraordinary. His huge work was further assembled in his contribution to the *Historia de Galicia* directed by Otero Pedrayo (1973), even though the original manuscript was from 1952 (LÓPEZ CUEVILLAS, 1973).

In the thirties, Georg and Vera Leisner travelled to Galicia. They were the authors of the foremost studious corpus on the megalithic culture of the Iberian Peninsula, i.e. the *Die Megalithgräber der Iberischen Halbinsel*, joined by several large volumes published in 1943, 1956, 1959 1965, and a posthumous tome in 1998. As far as Galicia is concerned, in 1938 G. Leisner published his doctoral thesis, entitled *Verbreitung und Typologie der Galizish-Nordportugiesischen Megalithgräber*. This was to be the fundamental work of the moment, together with his magnificent article on Pedra Cuberta, one of the most famous European megaliths with paintings (LEISNER, 1934). The Leisners' work was based on an exhaustive work of prospection, a magnificent planimetry, a thorough study of the archaeological materials and a valuable body of documentation. Besides, their theoretical contribution must be underlined. They managed to balance the diffusionist paradigm with the possibility of independent developments, thus avoiding the excessively simplistic evolutionary theories of the time. No doubt, theirs was a chief labour to which we still have to resort in our current approaches to the megalithic culture of the Iberian Peninsula. In this sense, as stated by W. Dehn in the opening of the congress organized in 1985 in Lisbon as a tribute to V. Leisner: "The catalogues of monuments and the typology of burial structures, the descriptions of the burial practices, the discussion of the grave goods, the intuition of the possible chronological sequence of the cultural groups and, finally, the exposition of the specific research case may be considered as the typical characteristics of the Leisners' work on megalithic culture" (DEHN, 1990, p. 12).

Both in the works by the Leisners and by López Cuevillas we find another interpretative approach: the hypothesis of a geological and topographical determinism. In several publications they emphasized over and over again the link between the spatial settings of the monuments and the granite substrates, as already expounded by G. Leisner as early as 1938. In addition, they realized how the barrows would appear mostly – even if not exclusively – in mountain passes and terminal plains of mountain ranges, in contrast to lower areas and valleys where, due to agricultural activities, many sites may have been destroyed (LÓPEZ CUEVILLAS, 1973, p. 55).

All three Macineira, G. Leisner and Cuevillas presented pioneer typological analyses. The former identified in the district of Ortegal three main categories: simple dolmen, passage grave and cist. According to Cuevillas, Galician monuments could be classified in four types (LÓPEZ CUEVILLAS, 1973, p. 58), as follows:

– Closed polygonal chambers of small size.
– Simple polygonal chambers with an open access.
– Polygonal chambers with a tendency towards the circular shape and a short passage.
– Rectangular chambers of the type of megalithic cists.

Based on this general scheme, G. Leisner broadly followed Cuevillas's typology, even though he perfected it by drawing from his own fieldwork (LEISNER, 1938, p. 18-34). Hence he distinguishes three groups:

– Simple tombs, with different types of chambers.
– Passage graves, differentiated both in profile and in plan, or with profile in steps.
– Semicircular chambers.

In a broad sense (Fig. 2), these typological analyses are the foundations of the most recent chrono-typological seriations (i.e. FÁBREGAS, 1988; CRIADO & FÁBREGAS, 1989; BELLO, 1996a; RODRÍGUEZ CASAL, 1990, 1997, 1999). This fact itself indicates the value and interest of the research of those brilliant archaeologists.

After the dismantling of the Seminario de Estudos Galegos with the political repression subsequent to the Civil War, and following to the creation of the Instituto "Padre Sarmiento" de Estudios Gallegos in 1944, a good number of scholars will resume archaeological research. Together with López Cuevillas's work, we have to point out the prospection and excavations by Ramón Sobrino in Morrazo. This period coincides with the celebration in Galicia of the 3rd National Congress of Archaeology. Although of relative value, we may also mention the work by F. Bouza Brey, A. Fraguas, J. Mª Luengo, M.Vázquez Seijas (RODRÍGUEZ CASAL, 1993, p. 65, notes 27 and 28) and, above all, the publication of the first catalogues of megaliths of the province of Pontevedra (FILGUEIRA & GARCÍA-ALÉN, 1977).

Once in the sixties, certain changes in the mentalities and in the approach to megaliths start to be identified. This may be related to the general shift taking place in Western Europe. Even though the number of fieldwork projects is limited at this time, we can mention the catalogues of megaliths in the district of Compostela and A. Blanco Freijeiro's study of the "Lapa de Gargantáns", one of the few menhirs known in Galicia.

3. FROM THE "CLASSICS' LESSON" TO THE COMPILATIONS OF THE GALICIAN MEGALITHIC CULTURE IN 1990.

From the seventies onwards, the amount of prospection and excavation projects increased significantly. The University of Santiago, the Instituto "Padre Sarmiento" de Estudios Gallegos and the archaeological museums of the different provinces coordinated a series of projects.

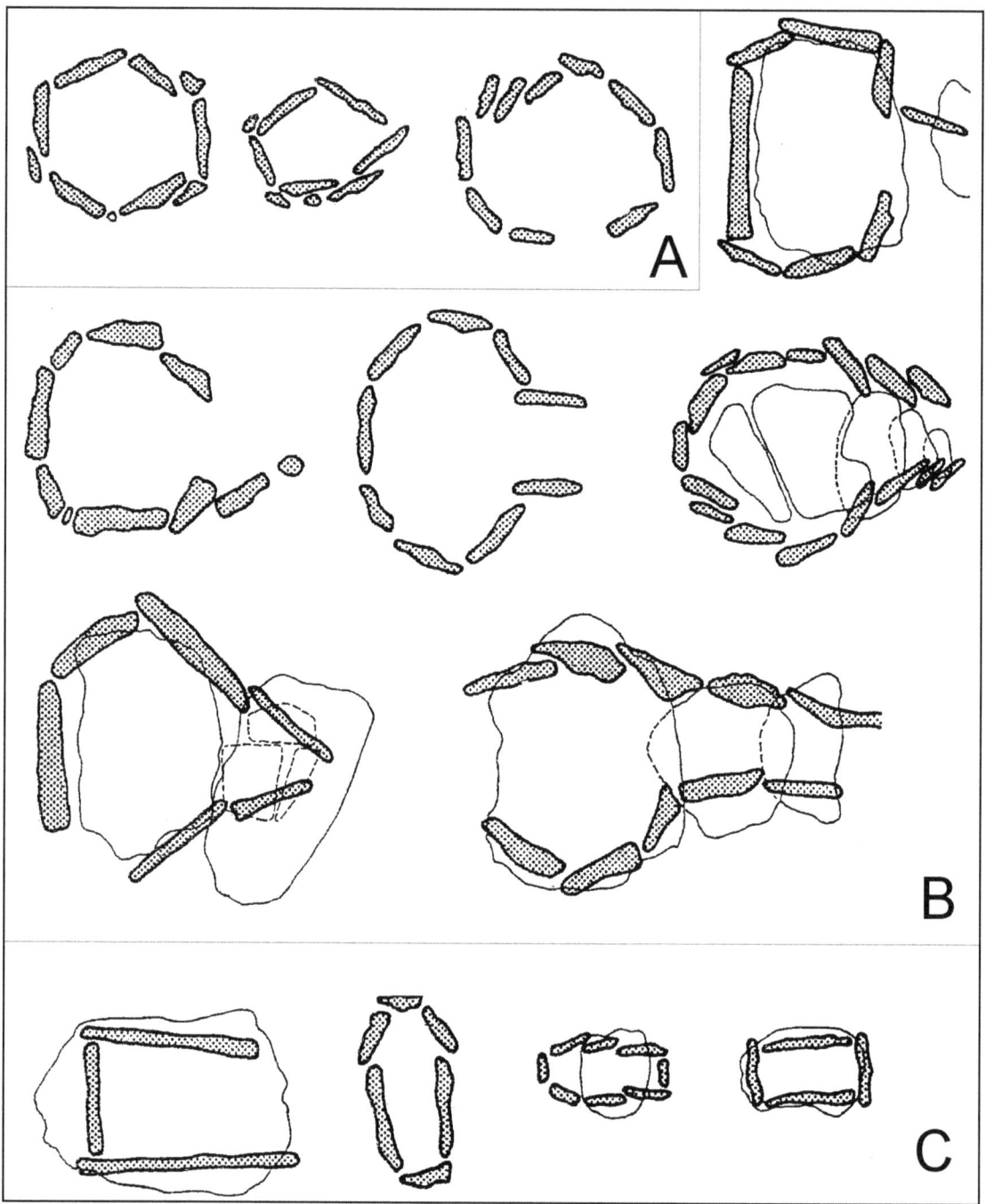

Figure 2. Typology of Galician megalithic monuments. A. Polygonal single-tombs. B. Passage-graves. C. Rectangular cists.

Especially relevant were the publication of the inventory of megalithic monuments of the province of Pontevedra (FILGUEIRA & GARCÍA-ALÉN, 1977), the excavations at Lousada (BOUZA et al., 1973), and several studies on megalithic art (SHEE & GARCÍA MARTÍNEZ, 1973; SAVORY, 1973; RAMIL et al., 1976). In the end of this decade, several syntheses were published which compiled the state of affairs up to that point (RODRÍGUEZ CASAL, 1979; VV.AA., 1979).

The eighties were the "prodigious decade" for the research on megaliths in Galicia. Firstly, numerous campaigns of prospection started in different districts, from Xallas and Barbanza to Fonsagrada, or from As Pontes de García Rodríguez to southern Ourense. Furthermore, many excavations undertaken in this period would have a crucial influence in subsequent studies: for instance, the work carried out in O Morrazo, the area of Vigo, Parxubeira, Os Campiños, Monte Campelos, Fanegas, Dombate, As Pontes...

Moreover, this boost in the research activity was characterized by a new methodological approach, as discussed in 1981 at the 2nd Seminar of Prehistory of the Northwest. In this meeting, researchers agreed that the study of the megalithic culture could not be separated from the environment. Rather, it should be approached as a double system of relationships, i.e. between ecology and culture. Within this framework, we can mention the projects carried out at the Sierra de Barbanza (AIRA *et al.*, 1986), the reconsideration of the megalithic culture in the province of A Coruña (BELLO *et al.*, 1987) and several works by F. Criado and his collaborators (CRIADO, 1980, 1988; CRIADO & GRAJAL, 1981). In addition, it is worthwhile pointing out the new approach to the material culture of megalith builders, due to authors such as J. Mª Eguileta (EGUILETA, 1987), F. de la Fuente (FUENTE, 1988) and, above all, R. Fábregas, who accomplished an integral study of the lithic industries (FÁBREGAS, 1991).

As regards the symbolic world of the megalithic culture, when E. Shee published his compilation on the megalithic art of Western Europe, she already dealt with seven Galician sites (SHEE, 1981). Her work would be the foundation for several subsequent studies. Additionally, in the late eighties, the excavation of the dolmen of Dombate started. This, together with the publication stemmed from the fieldwork undertaken in Parxubeira (1977-1984), shall determine the later evolution of Galician studies of megaliths. Parxubeira and Dombate are the two monuments which best allow a chronological sequence of the megalithic culture.

The megalithic site of A Parxubeira was excavated by A. Rodríguez Casal between 1977 and 1984 (RODRÍGUEZ CASAL, 1989). The study of the materials recovered led to the definition of three main periods of activity, as follows (Fig. 3):

a) Primary activity: with microliths, flint blades, arrowheads with a triangular base, polished axes, hoes, impressed pottery and variscite beads: Chronology: ca. 3500 BC.

b) Chalcolithic activity: with international style bell beakers, lineal variety, dotted-geometrical style and impressed with shell. Chronology: ca. 2300-1900 BC.

c) Early Bronze Age activity: represented by a flat-bottomed pot and copper arrowheads of the Palmela type. Chronology: ca. 1800 BC.

In addition, as a result of the research directed by A. Rodríguez Casal, there is another relevant element now well contextualized: i.e. the series of anthropomorphic steles in granite plaques and idols in pebble stones. They were all found at the entrance of the passage, just in the periphery of the tumulus. According to the stratigraphy, these artefacts are to be dated to the earliest phase of the monument construction. As to their meaning, they are understood as anthropomorphic representations of the Neolithic deity of the death (RODRÍGUEZ CASAL, 1998, p.80). In other words, these images would preside and defend the funerary space, as landmarks between the inner and outer side of the monuments, between life and death. (BUENO & BALBÍN, 1997, p. 703).

The second foremost megalithic site in Galicia is the dolmen of Dombate, already known in the 19th century through the famous poem by the bard Eduardo Pondal. It was after one century that the monument came into light again, now thanks to the archaeological work carried out by José María Bello since 1987. According to this researcher, "the excavation of the passage grave of Dombate provided new elements for the definition of the megalithic apogee in Galicia; among them, we may mention the verification of the superposition of two monuments at the same setting, the considerable monumentality of the more recent megalith, and the discovery, at the entrance area, of a row of 17 small idols standing *in situ*, together with another three which were in secondary position. The study of the artefacts in their archaeological context allows the hypothesis of a chronological sequence in the life of the monument: there are four moments that radiocarbon methods (both traditional and AMS) dated to 3700-2500 cal BC (4900-4000 BP). The inside of the megalithic structure shows important representations of parietal art, not only engravings (…) but also paintings (...). This, together with the monumentality of Dombate and the degree of social development of the society that built it, brings up an idea of the megalithic culture in Galicia which is very different from the traditional picture of it as poor, marginal, late and scarcely monumental" (BELLO, 1996b, p. 23). In the present day, Dombate is again recovering social notoriety, due to an ongoing ambitious project of conservation (BELLO, CARRERA & CEBRIÁN, 1997).

Following the classic authors - mainly the Leisners and López Cuevillas – and after the research boost of the eighties, two works of synthesis of the megalithic culture of Galicia were published in 1990. Both of them, written by A. Rodríguez Casal, came as a counterpoint of that published by F. Criado and R. Fábregas one year before (CRIADO y FÁBREGAS, 1989). The first one appeared in the volume published as a tribute to Dr. Vera Leisner. It focuses on the three main features of the megalithic culture in Galicia: the situation of the region in one of the Atlantic finisterrae, the antiquity of the complex and the distribution pattern of the monuments all across the country. These elements make Galicia's megalithic culture particularly interesting within the framework of the Atlantic façade. (RODRÍGUEZ CASAL, 1990a, p. 53). The second book, published by the University of Santiago de Compostela under the suggestive title "the earliest monumental architecture of Galicia" (RODRÍGUEZ CASAL, 1990b), compiled all the research on megaliths carried out until that moment.

4. THE LAST DECADE OF THE 20TH CENTURY AND THE STATE OF RESEARCH AT THE DAWN OF THE NEW MILLENIUM

The nineties started with a series of publications that placed the Galician megalithic culture in the right place within the peninsular and Atlantic context (FÁBREGAS, 1991; CRIADO & FÁBREGAS, 1994; RAMIL, ed., 1996). Besides, the number of publications on megalithic art increased, as a result of new research in Argalo, Parxubeira, Dombate, Forno dos Mouros or Mota Grande (BUENO & BALBÍN, 1992; RODRÍGUEZ CASAL, 1992 y 1998; FÁBREGAS, 1993; VÁZQUEZ VARELA, 1993; BELLO, 1994, 1995, 1996). Just as the celebration of the 3rd International Colloquium of Megalithic Art in A

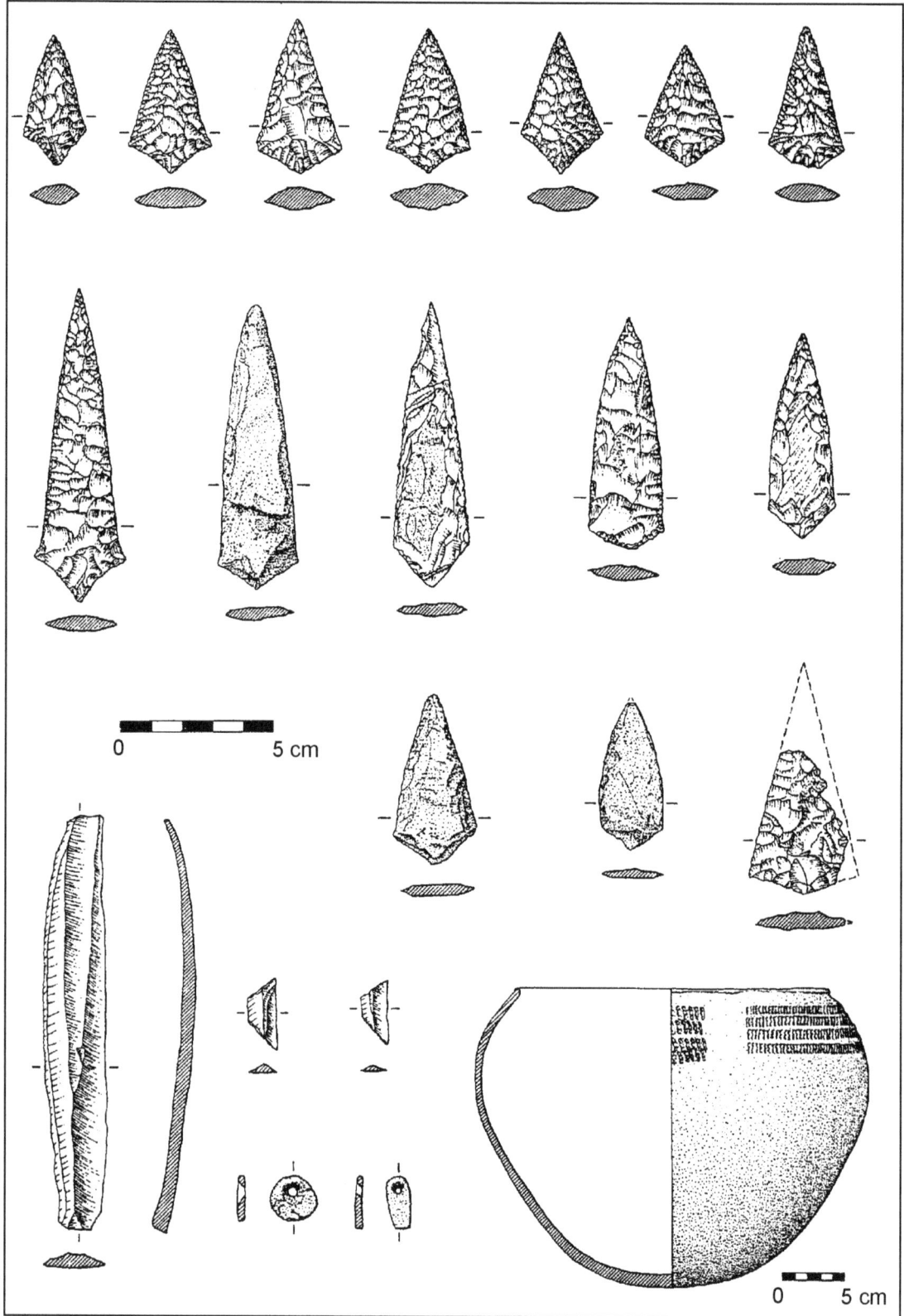

Figure 3. Grave goods from the megalithic necropolis of Parxubeira (Primary horizon).

Coruña in 1997 was very important (VV.AA., 1997), so was the event celebrated the year before in Santiago de Compostela: The Atlantic Neolithic and the Origins of Megaliths (RODRÍGUEZ CASAL, ed., 1997). This congress allowed the presentation of the megalithic culture of Galicia to the international scientific community, during a scientific meeting characterized by the lively debates.

Unfortunately, systematic archaeological excavations have been scanty during the nineties (VILASECO, 2001). This is mainly due to the Galician Government harmful archaeological policy, which limits the development of research. For this reason, we still have to rely on the data from the excavations undertaken during the last decade, such as Parxubeira (RODRÍGUEZ CASAL, 1989), Os

Campiños (FÁBREGAS & FUENTE, 1991-1992), Peinador-Galiñeiro (ABAD, 1992-1993, 1995; cf. GÓMEZ NISTAL & RODRÍGUEZ CASAL, 2000; GÓMEZ NISTAL, 2001), Dombate (BELLO, 1994, 1995, 1996), the study of A Baixa Limia by J. Mª Eguileta (EGUILETA, 1993-1994, 1997,1999), or the work at the Dorsal Meridiana Gallega and As Pontes by J. Vaquero (VAQUERO, 1999), among the most relevant.

On the other hand, some researchers of megaliths that were very promising during the eighties, such as Felipe Criado Boado and his Research Unit in Landscape Archaeology, have progressively abandoned the study of megaliths (e.g. among the last publications: CRIADO & VAQUERO, 1991; CRIADO & VAQUERO, 1993; CRIADO & VILLOCH, 1998). Instead, their current interests are theoretical archaeology (CRIADO, 1989), spatial archaeology and public archaeology, in line with the policy supported by the Galician Government. This policy seems to neglect the true essence of archaeology, that is, the systematic excavation understood as the fundamental tool which enables the historical reconstruction of the past.

5. PRESENT AND FUTURE OF THE MEGALITHIC RESEARCH IN GALICIA

Bearing in mind the need for revising the current research approaches, in 1993 we founded the Research Group "Archaeology and Ecology of the Megalithic Culture in Galicia" (http://www.usc.es/arqmega) aiming at an integral study of the complex. The group is organized in accordance to four main concerns: assessment of the available information, intensive prospection and excavation of the most representative sites and management of the megalithic heritage.

On the one hand, one objective was the accomplishment of a thorough review of all the available documentary and historiographical information. There were many hints at the importance of the documentation dating from the Middle Ages to the 19th century that needed to be investigated. On the other hand, it was considered as a priority to start an intensive campaign of prospection. The old distribution maps of megaliths exhibited substantial blanks which were mainly due to the lack of research, together with the historical destruction of monuments.

The megalithic culture of the coastal areas of Galicia was reasonably well documented, as seen in the publications on the current provinces of A Coruña (BELLO et al., 1987) and Pontevedra (FILGUEIRA y GARCÍA ALÉN, 1977). However, our knowledge about the interior was very fragmentary, with only some remarkable exceptions such as the research by J. M. Eguileta in Baixa Limia, Ourense (EGUILETA, 1999) and other minor studies in the province of Lugo. As a result, the megalithic culture of the interior was traditionally considered as marginal within the context of Galicia. For these reasons, when we designed a major research project, we decided to start by surveying the interior province of Lugo, before extending the study into the southern regions, i.e. the province of Ourense and the south of Pontevedra. The project would conclude with the prospection of the northwestern districts. Eventually, a global view of the megalithic culture of Galicia would be achieved.

At this stage of our research, we can provide some unpublished aspects of the results yielded by the project in the province of Lugo. Some advances had already been published in the 1996 congress (RODRIGUEZ CASAL et al., 1997). Currently, the database amounts to more than one thousand monuments catalogued, together with studies of soils from the tumuli and petrographic analyses.

5.1. Lugo as a test tube: figures and monuments

Across its 10000 km², the province of Lugo shows a great geomorphologic diversity, with very distinct and well-defined landscapes. At the present moment, we have catalogued 1027 barrows, all of them studied on site (Fig. 4). Each and every monument is registered in a record file with the geographic coordinates and several aspects as to their morphology and structures, as well as indications with regards to hydrology, edafology, geology, visibility and environment.

Even though it can be said that these monuments generally fall within the common ranges of volume and composition, we have located some of extraordinary size, with diameters over 50 m and heights around 4 m, with volumes exceeding 4000 m³. The most outstanding case is one monument in Castro de Rei with more than 6000 m³ of earth and diameters over 60 m. In addition, we have located several clusters of megaliths concentrated in small areas. Among them, we may underline the group of Monte de Santa Mariña, with thirty burial monuments in a very limited surface (Fig. 5).

Founded on the database, we have performed several inductive statistical analyses from the SPSS. The contingency tables – up to 16 have been designed – allow the evaluation of the degree of association between two qualitative variables. In one case, for example, when we relate the data from the monuments' morphology to the orography, we verify statistically the mutual refusal between those barrows with lithic cuirasse and those placed in open valleys. In addition, we notice that the former ones tend to appear in mountain passes.

Another contingency table, which measures the association between monument composition and physical environment, showed a predominance of tumuli with lithic cuirasse on mountain tops and hillside settings. The explanation to this phenomenon hitherto given by some Galician archaeologists was of a symbolic nature: those monuments with well-structured lithic cuirasses would be placed on tops in order to be seen from the distance. However, we can also offer an explanation of a functional nature. In our view, some factors such as weathering should be borne in mind. Wind and rain weathering phenomena are very strong in high and steep areas, which might have resulted in these monuments exhibiting their lithic cuirasses. On the contrary, the biggest monuments in terms of earth appear in valleys, i.e. where the soil is deeper and hence it is more easily available. There are some exceptions to this pattern:

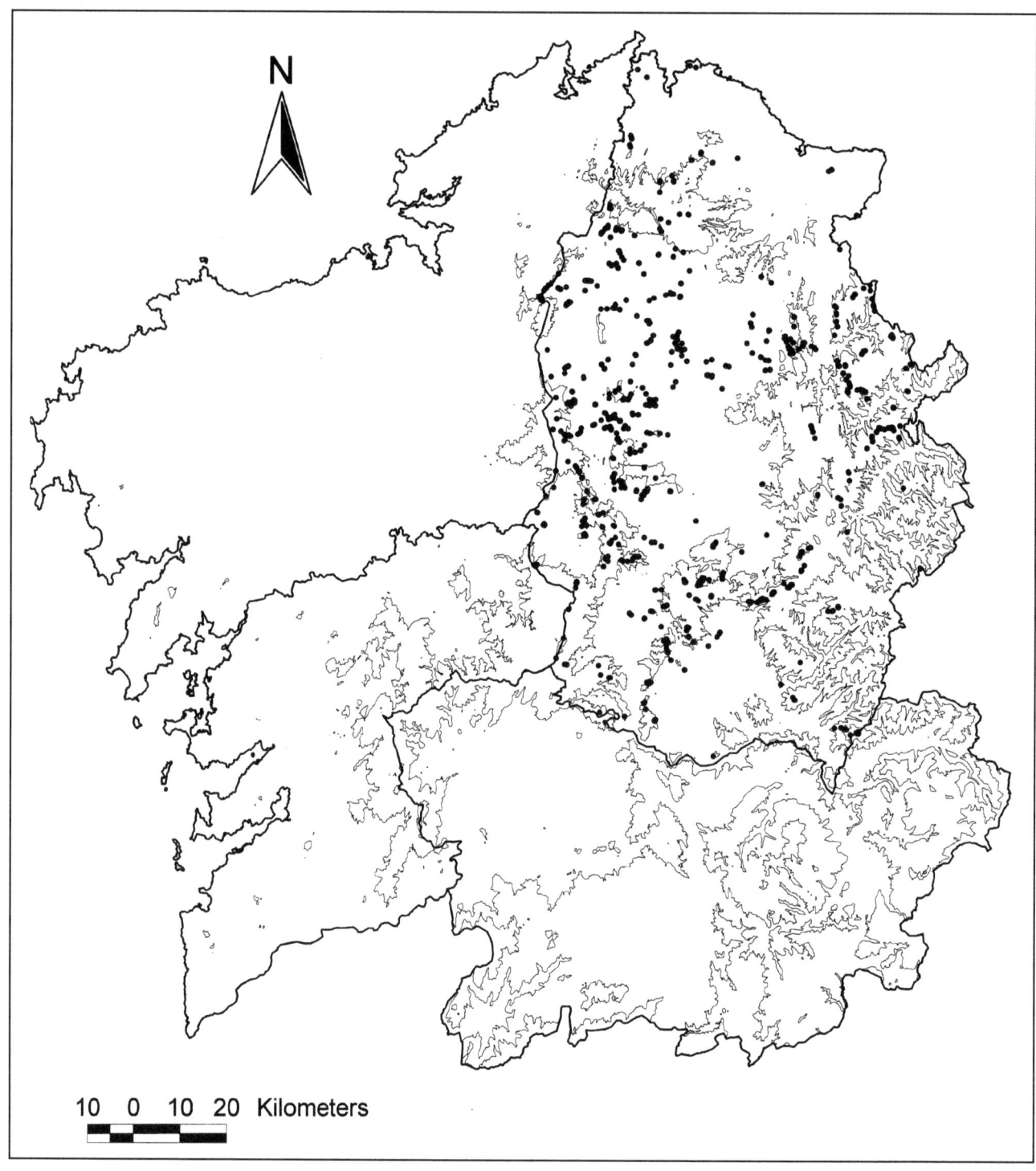

Figure 4. Megalithic distribution in the province of Lugo at the present day. (Compare to figure 1).

the megalithic group of the valley of Maus de Salas (Ourense), shows monuments with very well preserved, clean and shiny lithic cuirasses. To be seen from the distance? Far from that, the explanation is simple and has little to do with symbolic aspects. This necropolis had been covered by a hydroelectric reservoir. Therefore, all remains of soil had been washed away.

5.1.1. Soils and tumuli: edafologic observations

Even though there is a considerable amount of information about the palinology of megaliths' soils, there is a lack of studies of edafology (AIRA *et al.*, 1989). This research gap was emphasized during the congress on "The Atlantic Neolithic and the Origins of Megaliths", celebrated in Santiago de Compostela in 1996 (MARTÍNEZ CORTIZAS, 1997). Consequently, together with the archaeological prospection, our team conducted analyses of more than one hundred samples of sediments from different tumuli of 29 sites.

The first obstacle that we had to overcome was the lack of detailed maps of soils and lithology, not only for Lugo but for the entire Galicia. Furthermore, another problem was

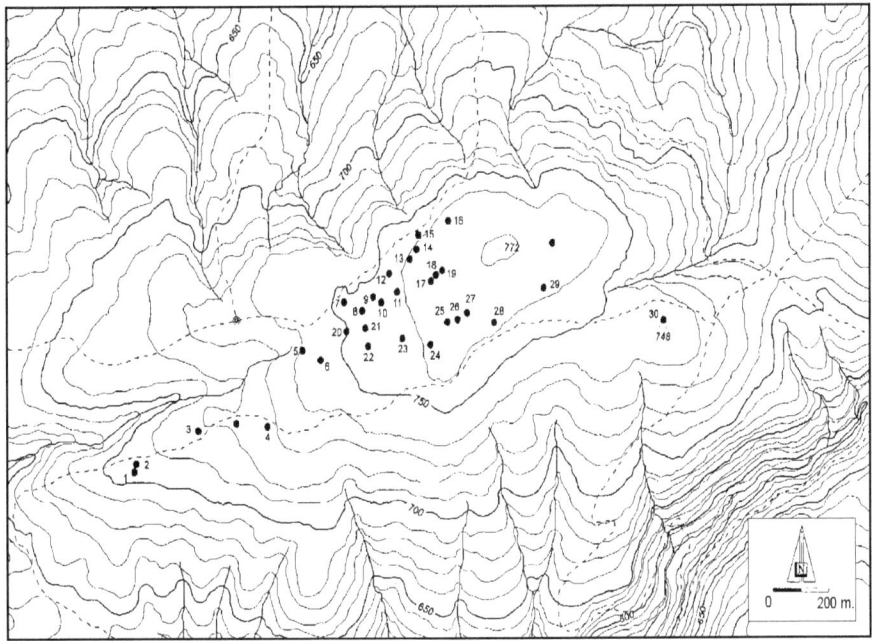

Figure 5. Megalithic grouping of Monte de Santa Mariña, one of the most impressive in Galicia.

the "presentist" approach to the scarce maps available. In other words, the soils that we find nowadays surrounding a monument may be anything from very similar to absolutely different from those existing 5000 years ago. This may be due to both anthropic and natural processes. Besides, the transformations in the landscape may be much more recent than the megalithic constructions. Given that most of the monuments are erected in high settings, weathering processes may have exerted a dramatic influence. Instead, in the opposite case, in low or accumulative lands, we find soils of the type "Atlantic ranker", with sediment deposits over 1 m deep, sometimes 7000 to 5000 years old.

In 1982, the edafologic analysis of one tumulus of A Parxubeira was published. From this study, several interesting deductions were made. The analytical data suggested that "the earth at the base of the tumulus comes from the dismantlement of the 'A' horizons (palaeosoil) of those soils adjacent to the barrow, whereas the earth of the upper layers of the mound had been taken from the lower horizons of that same soil". In this case, the monument displayed an "upturned stratigraphy" in relation to the surrounding natural soil (CALVO, CRIADO & VÁZQUEZ, 1982, p. 72-74).

Such facts, however, cannot be considered as a general rule that applies to all megaliths. Granulometric analyses or studies of the organic carbon content of samples from monuments in Lugo show both uniformity and heterogeneity, depending on particular cases. For example, the analyses of the soils from Santa Mariña exhibited a significant homogeny, whereas the amount of clay in the samples from Bardaos and A Millarada varied significantly from one tumulus to another. Accordingly, we have to emphasize that each site has its own edafologic history, and hence we cannot study the construction of barrows within tight frameworks.

Another research concern is how to assess reliably the evolution of the soils throughout the last 5000-6000 years. Even though the general edafogenesis may have not changed much, environmental changes may have caused important modifications: for instance, the variation of temperature and humidity, and hence of the vegetation, may have accentuated weathering processes (e.g. increase of inorganic materials in peat bogs). Also human activities may have altered the soils significantly.

5.1.2. Rocks and barrows: geological observations

The characteristic geology of Lugo makes it a privileged scenario for the study of the relationship between the materials of the subsoil and the other variables recorded from the megaliths. The study of the 132 megalithic structures preserved and the statistical analyses of the results led to interesting conclusions that challenge some theories hitherto accepted.

To begin with, we may point out the preference shown in the use of granite and quartzite materials for the megalithic constructions. In all the megaliths set on granite substrates, this was the material used for the structure. Even in those cases of megaliths placed on different substrates, still 14% of them were built with granite. This implies certain degree of transport.

As far as quartzite materials are concerned, the trend is similar. Out of the monuments set on quartzite substrates, 87% were made of quartzite. Even though this percent is not as radical as that from the granite monuments, it is remarkably higher than those from other types of rocks (slate 74%, schist 69%, basic rocks 66%, sediments 10%).

On the other hand, it appears obvious that megalith builders refused to make use of sedimentary rocks. Only

0,7% of the megalithic structures from Lugo were made of such, in spite of 15% of them being erected in zones of sediments. The only identified sample of a slab of sedimentary rock (Sample No. 4, M1 of A Chá) had initially been classified as a quartzite with a low degree of metamorphism, however the thin section indicated that it was a very compact sandstone with calcareous cement. This fact is strange and singular, as we would rarely expect such material being used for a megalithic structure. In this case, the petrographic analysis allowed the detection of an error of classification. In addition, it enabled us to correct the transportation distance initially supposed for this monument. The source of this rock was in the surroundings of the monument, whereas the nearest outcrop of quartzite was about 2 km far. Finally, we may state that in no case we found a source of stone further than 1,5/2 km from the monument. Moreover, they are normally found within a few hundred metres of the megalithic structure.

It seems, therefore, that the mechanical quality of the rocks (resistance, hardness, tenacity) was the main reason behind their choice in each particular case. This idea is further strengthened by the pattern of use of slate and schist, more fragile: these types of geological substrates are present in about 60% of the province, and indeed these rocks are often used for megalithic structures. Nevertheless, almost one third of the megaliths placed on these substrates were built with granite or quartzite obtained elsewhere.

The facts explained above are indicative of the pragmatism of the megalith builders in the interior of Galicia. In the choice of raw materials, it seems that the equation material-economy of effort was solved by maximizing possibilities, i.e. using the most suitable materials within limited margins of effort.

5.1.3. On the statistical relationship between outcrop/subsoil and monumentality

Out of all the monuments catalogued, we have been able to perform statistical analyses of 592, taking only those cases where the measurements and volume estimations were reliable. The sample is thus relatively wide and representative. The results are as follows (Table 1):

Table 1.

Volume (m³)	Percent
0-25	1.01 %
25-300	76.52%
300-500	14.02
500-1000	7.43 %
>1000	1.52 %

Table 1 shows that most of the monuments, namely 77,53 % of them, are smaller than 300 m³, and only 1,5% (10 barrows) reach over 1000 m³. The average volume is 262 m³.

It is also interesting to address the volumetric data and relate them to the various substrates on which the monuments are placed (Table 2).

The data presented in tables 1 and 2 lead to one clear conclusion: barrows show bigger volumes in those settings where the soils are – or are likely to have been – deeper. As earth is the fundamental raw material used to build these monuments, it seems that the availability of this material was the main factor determining the erection of bigger tumuli.

Thus, monumentality would be basically related to the possibility of getting suitable materials, that is to say, to the characteristics of the substrate. In any case, we have to bear in mind that all the figures used for the volumes have been calculated in accordance with the present condition of the monuments. Many monuments may have lost considerable amounts of their sediments through history, due to both natural and anthropic reasons. Therefore, once again we have to encourage caution in these "presentist" approaches.

In this sense, it may appear striking the lack of a clear association between dimensions of the tumuli and current depth of the soils. The possible reasons behind this fact are various. Firstly, this may be due to the fact that the current depth of the soil is not the same as it was 5000 years ago. Secondly, it is feasible that this was not a decisive factor in the choice of a particular setting for a monument. Thirdly, perhaps the construction of the monument itself may have altered the state of the soil. If a big tumulus was built in an areas with relatively shallow soils (e.g. the enormous tumulus of A Mota Grande in Sierra do Leboreiro), the hundreds of cubic metres of earth needed would mean the dismantlement of A and B horizons in the surrounding land. Hence weathering would have been much more intense. Lastly, not only the depth of the soils but also the vegetation may have changed considerably. Therefore the vegetation should only very cautiously be taken as indicative of the depth of the soil, when trying to reconstruct prehistoric landscapes.

Even if the factors conditioning the setting of megaliths in Lugo – and in the entire Galicia – are various (geographical, geological, economic or social), there is little doubt that the geological has to be considered as the main one. The relationship between raw material and monument setting seems to be the strongest. In this sense, we agree with Jean L'Helgouac'h, who wrote in 1965 an idea referred to Armorican megaliths which also applies to the Galician case scenario: "No civilization was more dependant on the nature of the subsoil than that of the megalith builders (...). It is unquestionable that the subsoil has considerably influenced the general distribution of megaliths".

6. EPILOGUE

As we have seen, the first area studied by our research team has been the province of Lugo. Despite that it was traditionally considered as a marginal zone, more than one

Table 2.

Granite	Min. volume: 18 m³ Average: 233 m³ Max. volume: 1420 m³	Those tumuli set on quartzite or sediments show volume values significantly above the general average. The sample of basic rocks cannot be considered as representative, for there were only two cases. In the other three possibilities (i.e. granite, slate, schist), the average volume values are similar among them, all of them below the general average. The biggest monument is placed on an outcrop of quartzite and is extraordinary. If the average is recalculated without this, then we obtain 239 m³, that is, a volume which is very similar to those values from non-sedimentary rocks. This is more consistent with its statistical representation. The biggest tumuli are mostly placed on sedimentary rocks, as indicated by the average volume.
Slate	Min. volume: 29 m³ Average: 199 m³ Max. volume: 723 m³	
Schist	Min. volume: 26 m³ Average: 213 m³ Max. volume: 990 m³	
Quartzite	Min volume: 35 m³ Average: 239 m³ Min. volume: 3927 m³	
Sediments	Min. volume: 28 m³ Average: 355 m³ Max. volume: 3141m³	
Basic rocks	Min. volume: 32 m³ Average: 67 m³ Max. volume: 102 m³	

thousand megaliths have already been catalogued. While statistical and interpretative analyses of the first results are undertaken, the fieldwork is now focused in the south of Galicia, where about seven hundred monuments have already been studied. The database will be completed with the prospection to be carried out in the north of Pontevedra and A Coruña. Thus, we aim to obtain a broad corpus of objective and scientifically verifiable data, which may enable us to address the megalithic culture of Galicia from a holistic perspective, in contrast to previous studies of a partial nature. The philosophy of our team is founded in a basic principle: it is impossible to formulate interpretations without a previous systematic and complete collection of information. This way, in following years we hope to be in a position to offer the first integral study of the Galician megalithic culture. As said by Santiago Ramón y Cajal, "the facts, if well observed, will last, regardless of changing interpretations".

A next stage will involve excavations at a series of representative sites, in order to further improve our knowledge of the megalithic complex and develop plans of protection and dissemination of the Galician megalithic richness. In short, objective record of information, systematic excavation, scientific analysis of data, and protection and dissemination of the megalithic heritage, are the focal points of our ongoing interdisciplinary project, devoted to the study of a cultural phenomenon rooted in the dawn of the fourth millennium BC.

Acknowledgements

I would like to thank my colleagues of the Research Group 0-38-5 of the University of Santiago de Compostela: José María Eguileta Franco, Elbio Ramos Albite, Carmen Gómez Nistal, Emiliana Romaní Fariña and Alfredo Iglesias Diéguez. I am also grateful to Eduardo García Rodeja and Carlota García Paz, from the Department of Edafology and Agricultural Chemistry of the Faculty of Biology of the University of Santiago de Compostela. Thanks are also due to Marcos Martinón-Torres for his help with the translation of the original manuscript.

Author's Address

Antón A. RODRÍGUEZ CASAL
Departamento de Historia I
Universidade de Santiago de Compostela
15703 Santiago de Compostela (Galicia, Spain)

Bibliography

ABAD GALLEGO, X.C., 1992-1993, Balance de las actuaciones arqueológicas llevadas a cabo en la necrópolis megalítica de Cotogrande (campañas de 1989-1992). *Castrelos* 5-6, p. 7-28.

ABAD GALLEGO, X.C., 1995, La variabilidad en las estructuras funerarias tumulares del noroeste peninsular: el ejemplo de la gran necrópolis Peinador-Galiñeiro. In *XXII Congreso Nacional de Arqueología*, vol. I, p. 391-398. Zaragoza.

AIRA, Mª J., CRIADO BOADO, F., & DÍAZ-FIERROS, F., 1986, *La construcción del paisaje: Megalitismo y ecología en la Sierra de Barbanza (Galicia)*. Santiago de Compostela: Xunta de Galicia.

AIRA, Mª J., SAA OTERO, P. & TABOADA CASTRO, T., 1989, *Estudios Paleobotánicos y Edafológicos en yacimientos arqueológicos de Galicia*. Santiago de Compostela: Xunta de Galicia.

BELLO DIÉGUEZ, J. Mª., 1994, Grabados, pinturas e ídolos en Dombate (Cabana, La Coruña). ¿Grupo de Viseu o grupo noroccidental? Aspectos taxonómicos y cronológicos". In *O Megalitismo no Centro de Portugal*, pp. 287-304. Viseu.

BELLO DIÉGUEZ, J. Mª., 1995: Arquitectura, arte parietal y manifestaciones escultóricas en el megalitismo noroccidental. In *Arqueoloxía e arte na Galicia prehistórica e romana*, p. 31-98. A Coruña: Gráficas do Castro/Moret.

BELLO DIÉGUEZ, J. Mª., 1996a, Arquitectura megalítica. In *El Fenómeno Megalítico en Galicia*, edited by E. Ramil Rego. Vilalba (Lugo): Servicio de Publicacións do Museu de Prehistoria e Arqueoloxía de Vilalba, p. 87-111.

BELLO DIÉGUEZ, J. Mª., 1996b, Aportaciones del dolmen de Dombate (Cabana, La Coruña) al arte megalítico occidental. *Révue Archéologique de l'Ouest*, supl. 8, p. 23-39.

BELLO DIÉGUEZ, J. Mª, CARRERA, F. & CEBRIÁN, F., 1997, El Proyecto de conservación del dolmen de Dombate. *Brigantium* 10, p. 393-408.

BELLO DIÉGUEZ, J. Mª, CRIADO BOADO, F. & VÁZQUEZ VARELA, J. M.,1987, *La Cultura megalítica de la provincia de La Coruña y sus relaciones con el marco natural: implicaciones socio-económicas*. A Coruña: Excma. Diputación Provincial.

BOUZA BREY, F., CARRO OTERO, J. & GARCÍA MARTÍNEZ, M.C.,1973,: Excavación de túmulos dolménicos en San Andrés de Lousada (Lugo). *Noticiario Arqueológico Hispánico* 2, p. 39-55.

BUENO, P. & BALBÍN BEHRMANN, R., 1992, L'art mégalithique dans la Péninsule Ibérique. Une vue d'ensemble. *L'Anthropologie* 93, 2-3, p. 499-572.

BUENO, P. & BALBÍN BEHRMANN, R., 1997, Ambiente funerario en la sociedad megalítica ibérica: Arte megalítico peninsular. In *O Neolítico Atlántico e as orixes do Megalitismo*, edited by Antón A. Rodríguez Casal. Santiago de Compostela: Servicio de Publicacións da Universidade de Santiago de Compostela, p. 693-718.

CALVO ANTA, R., CRIADO BOADO, F. & VÁZQUEZ VARELA, J. M., 1982, Contribución al estudio del Megalitismo y el medio edafológico en el Noroeste de la Península Ibérica: el paleosuelo de A mámoa de Parxubeira. *Cuadernos de Estudios Gallegos* 33, p. 65-87.

CRIADO BOADO, F., 1980, Catalogación de mámoas en los municipios de Curtis, Sobrado y tierras adyacentes. *Brigantium* 1, p. 13-40.

CRIADO BOADO, F., 1988, Arqueología del paisaje y espacio megalítico en Galicia. *Arqueología Espacial* 12, p. 61-117.

CRIADO BOADO, F., 1989, Megalitos, espacio y pensamiento. *Trabajos de Prehistoria* 46, p. 75-98.

CRIADO BOADO, F. & GRAJAL, M., 1981, Relación entre la distribución de mámoas y el medio físico en la zona de Sobrado-Curtis. *Brigantium* 2, p. 7-27.

CRIADO BOADO, F. & FÁBREGAS VALCARCE, R., 1989, Aspectos generales del Megalitismo galaico. *Arqueologia* 19, p.48-62. (English version in *Antiquity* 63, p. 682-696).

CRIADO BOADO, F. & FÁBREGAS VALCARCE, R., 1994, Regional patterning among the megaliths of Galicia (NW Spain). *Oxford Journal of Archaeology* 13.1, p. 33-47.

CRIADO BOADO, F. & VAQUERO LASTRES, J., 1991, El fenómeno megalítico y tumular: Formas diversas de pasado monumental. In *Arqueología del Paisaje. El área Bocelo-Furelos entre los tiempos paleolíticos y medievales*, directed by Felipe Criado Boado. Santiago de Compostela: Xunta de Galicia, p. 129-138.

DENH, W., 1990, Im Gedenken an Dr. h.c. Vera Leisner. In *Probleme der Megalithgräberforschung (Vorträge zum 100 Geburtstag von Vera Leisner)*. Berlin, New York: Walter de Gruyter, Madrider Forschungen, Bd. 16, p. 9-13.

EGUILETA FRANCO, J. Mª., 1987, Catálogo dos materiais ergolóxicos depositados no museo de Ourense procedentes de túmulos prehistóricos". *Boletín Auriense* 17, p. 9-98.

EGUILETA FRANCO, J. Mª., 1993-94, As mámoas dos Concellos da Baixa Limia: aportación al catálogo de monumentos tumulares de la comarca". *Cuadernos de Estudios Gallegos* 41, p. 41-64.

EGUILETA FRANCO, J. Mª., 1997, Megalitos y coordenadas espaciales en la Baixa Limia Gallega: ¿una neolitización tardía en la Galicia interior?". In *O Neolítico Atlántico e as orixes do Megalitismo*, edited by Antón A. Rodríguez Casal. Santiago de Compostela: Servicio de Publicacións da Universidade de Santiago de Compostela, p. 553-571.

EGUILETA FRANCO, J. Mª., 1999, *A Baixa Limia na Prehistoria Recente. Arqueoloxía dunha Paisaxe na Galicia Interior*. Ourense: Excma. Diputación Provincial.

FÁBREGAS VALCARCE, R., 1988, Megalitismo de Galicia. *Trabalhos de Antropologia e Etnologia* 29, p. 57-77.

FÁBREGAS VALCARCE, R., 1991, *Megalitismo del Noroeste de la Península Ibérica. Tipología y secuencia de los materiales líticos*. Madrid: Universidad Nacional a Distancia.

-1993, Las representaciones de bulto redondo en el Megalitismo del noroeste. *Trabajos de Prehistoria* 50, p. 87-101.

FÁBREGAS VALCARCE, R. & FUENTE, A. de la, 1988, *Aproximaciones a la cultura material del Megalitismo gallego: la industria lítica pulimentada y el material cerámico*. Santiago de Compostela: Tórculo Artes Gráficas.

FÁBREGAS VALCARCE, R. & FUENTE, A. de la, 1991, Excavación da mámoa 6 de Os Campiños (Leiro, Rianxo). Campaña de 1984. *Brigantium* 7, p. 91-149.

FERNÁNDEZ IBÁÑEZ, C. & FÁBREGAS VALCARCE, R., 1996, Obermaier y la Prehistoria en el Noroeste de la Península Ibérica. In *"El Hombre Fósil" 80 años después*, edited by Alfonso Moure Romanillo. Santander: Servicio de Publicaciones de la Universidad de Cantabria, p. 99-126.

FILGUEIRA VALVERDE, J. & GARCÍA-ALÉN, A., 1977, Inventario de Monumentos megalíticos de la provincia de Pontevedra. *El Museo de Pontevedra* 31, p. 43-130.

GÓMEZ NISTAL, C., 2001, Neolitización y Megalitismo en el entorno de la Ría de Vigo: estado actual de la investigación. *Gallaecia* 20, p. 39-60.

GÓMEZ NISTAL, C. & RODRÍGUEZ CASAL, A.A., 2000, El fenómeno tumular y megalítico en la Galicia suroccidental: Aspectos historiográficos y estado actual de la investigación". In *Neolitizaçâo e Megalitismo da Península Ibérica*, edited by V. Oliveira Jorge. Porto, p. 321-335.

LEISNER, G., 1934, Die Malerein des dolmen Pedra Coberta. *Jahrbuch für Prähistoriche und Etnographische Kunst* 9, p. 23-44.

LEISNER, G., 1938, *Verbreitung und typologie der Galizish-Nordportugiesischen Megalithgräber*. Universität zu Marburg. München: J. B. Lind.

LEISNER, G. & V., 1956, 1959, *Die Megalithgräber der Iberischen Halbinsel* (Der Westen). Berlin: Madrider Forschungen, band 1/1.

LÓPEZ CUEVILLAS, F.,1973, A edade megalítica. In *Historia de Galicia*, III (Prehistoria), edited by R. Otero Pedrayo, p. 43-122. Buenos Aires.

MACIÑEIRA PARDO DE LAMA, F., 1929, Notable grupo de círculos líthicos y túmulos dolménicos de la cuenca superior del Eume. *Arquivos do Seminario de Estudos Galegos* 2, p.197-218

MACIÑEIRA PARDO DE LAMA, F., 1935, La distribución de las estaciones prehistóricas ortegalesas y sus características. *Boletín de la Real Academia Gallega* 22, pp.61-84.

MACIÑEIRA PARDO DE LAMA, F., 1944-1945, Túmulos prehistóricos. Inventario descriptivo de los 286 túmulos prehistóricos hasta ahora descubiertos en la avanzada comarca del cabo Ortegal. *Boletín de la Real Academia Gallega* 24, pp. 15-34.

MARTÍNEZ CORTIZAS, A., 1997, Conceptos estratigráficos y edáficos en contextos tumulares. In *O Neolítico Atlántico e as orixes do Megalitismo*, edited by Antón A. Rodríguez Casal. Santiago de Compostela: Servicio de Publicacións da Universidade de Santiago de Compostela, p. 73-91.

MARTINÓN-TORRES, M., 2000, Murguía e a Arqueoloxía galega. *Boletín da Real Academia Galega* 361, p. 221-244.

MARTINÓN-TORRES, M., 2001, *Os monumentos megalíticos despois do Megalitismo. Arqueoloxía e Historia dos megalitos galegos a través das fontes escritas (s. VI-s. XIX)*. Valga: Plana Artes Gráficas.

MARTINÓN-TORRES, M. & RODRÍGUEZ CASAL, A.A. (2000): "Aspectos historiográficos del Megalitismo gallego: de la documentación medieval al siglo XIX". In *Neolitização e Megalitismo da Península Ibérica*, p. 303-319. Porto.

RAMIL REGO, E. (ed), 1996, *El Fenómeno Megalítico en Galicia"*. Vilalba (Lugo): Servicio de Publicacións do Museu de Prehistoria e Arqueoloxía de Vilalba.

RAMIL SONEIRA, J., VÁZQUEZ VARELA, J. M. & VIDAL, J., 1976, Tres túmulos megalíticos con grabados en el término municipal de Vilalba (Lugo). *Gallaecia* 2, p. 87-93.

RODRÍGUEZ CASAL, A. A., 1979, O Megalitismo na Galiza. A súa problemática e o estado actual da investigación". In *O Neolítico e o Calcolítico em Portugal*. Porto, p. 103-115.

RODRÍGUEZ CASAL, A. A., 1989, *La necrópolis megalítica de Parxubeira (Campañas arqueológicas de 1977 a 1984)*. A Coruña: Gráficas do Castro/Moret.

RODRÍGUEZ CASAL, A. A., 1990a, Die Megalithkultur in Galicien. In *Probleme der Megalithgräberforschung (Vorträge zum 100 Geburtstag von Vera Leisner)*. Berlin, New York: Walter de Gruyter, Madrider Forschungen, Bd. 16, p. 53-77.

RODRÍGUEZ CASAL, A. A., 1990b, *O Megalitismo. A primeira arquitectura monumental de Galicia*. Santiago de Compostela: Servicio de Publicacións da Universidade de Santiago de Compostela.

RODRÍGUEZ CASAL, A. A., 1992, Elements symbolico-funeraires du Mégalithisme galicien. *Révue Archéologique de l'Ouest*, sup. 5, p. 213-221.

RODRÍGUEZ CASAL, A. A., 1993, "Análise historiográfica do Megalitismo galego. In *Galicia e a Historiografía*, edited by X. G. Beramendi. Santiago de Compostela: Tórculo Edicións, p. 53-71.

RODRÍGUEZ CASAL, A. A., 1997, Neolitización e Megalitismo en Galicia. In *O Neolítico Atlántico e as orixes do Megalitismo*, edited by Antón A. Rodríguez Casal. Santiago de Compostela: Servicio de Publicacións da Universidade de Santiago de Compostela, p. 447-462.

RODRÍGUEZ CASAL, A. A., 1998, Las estelas antropomorfas de Parxubeira en el contexto de la estatuaria megalítica del noroeste de la Península Ibérica. *Archéologie en Languedoc* 22, p.73-82.

RODRÍGUEZ CASAL, A. A., 1999, Le Mégalithisme en Galice. Tumulus, dolmens et rites funérarires. In *Mégalithismes de l'Atlantique à l'Ethiopie*, edited by Jean Guilaine. Paris: Éditions Errance, p. 91-106.

RODRÍGUEZ CASAL, A.A., EGUILETA FRANCO, J. Mª., GÓMEZ NISTAL, C., RAMOS ALBITE, E. & ROMANÍ FARIÑA, E., 1997, Metodología y primeras valoraciones de un proyecto interdisciplinar sobre el fenómeno tumular en la provincia de Lugo. In *O Neolítico Atlántico e as orixes do Megalitismo*, edited by Antón A. Rodríguez Casal. Santiago de Compostela: Servicio de Publicacións da Universidade de Santiago de Compostela, p. 521-536.

SAVORY, H. N., 1973, Serpentiforms in Megalithic art: a link between Wales and the Iberian North-West. *Cuadernos de Estudios Gallegos* 28, p. 80-89.

SHEE TWOHIG, E., 1981, *The Megalithic Art of Western Europe*. Oxford: Clarendon Press.

SHEE TWOHIG, E. & GARCÍA MARTÍNEZ, M.C.,1973, Tres tumbas megalíticas decoradas en Galicia. *Trabajos de Prehistoria* 30, p. 335-348.

VAQUERO LASTRES, J., 1999, *Les extrêmes distincts. La configuration de l'espace dans les sociétés ayant bâti des tertres funéraires dans le Nord-Ouest ibérique*. BAR International Series 821. Oxford.

VÁZQUEZ VARELA, J. M., 1993, "Arte Prehistórico". In *Arte Prehistórico y Romano*. A Coruña: Hércules Ediciones, p 21-233.

VILASECO VÁZQUEZ, X. I., 2001, As escavacións arqueolóxicas en monumentos tumulares de Galicia: 1965-1998. Cuestións metodolóxicas e bibliométricas. *Gallaecia* 20, p. 61-95.

VV.AA, 1979, *Prehistoria e Arqueoloxía de Galicia. Estado da cuestión*. Santiago de Compostela: Instituto "Padre Sarmiento" de Estudios Gallegos.

VV.AA., 1997, *III Coloquio Internacional de Arte megalítico*. (Brigantium 10). A Coruña: Vía Láctea S.L.

www.ingramcontent.com/pod-product-compliance
Ingram Content Group UK Ltd.
Pitfield, Milton Keynes, MK11 3LW, UK
UKHW061213180426
11947UKWH00029B/2034